Burning Desire

A Motivational: True story of how I beat the odds and became successful at selling Real Estate my first year in the business.

by

Deborah Ann Spence

SOLD it

DEBORAH
SPENCE

CONTENTS

Appendix

Notes

Acknowledgements

First, I like to dedicate this book to my Uncle David R. Lewis (1939-2008) for passing on to me the passion of writing to inspire others. I miss you so much and I hope I have made you proud.

There are so many people to thank who have helped me along the way in my journey of self-discovery, my success in real estate, and in writing this book.

I am thankful for my Mother, Rosemary Spence, who did the best that she could to raise us. I am grateful for the energy of my sister Dawn Michelle Spence (1962-2007) from whom I get the burning desire to move on and for my brothers—Peter, Paul, and Sean, who are always available to help me in my time of need. I thank my two sons, Naajee and Jahbulani, for giving me the inspiration to tell my story; my Aunt Patricia Lewis, who told me she would read about my success in the newspaper, and she did—3 months later. I thank my content editor Rich Mintzer for his endless patience and for sharing his enormous wealth of knowledge about writing, publishing, marketing, and more. I thank my Public Relations/editor, Eartha Watts Hicks for all of her hard work and relentless energy. I am especially thankful for my friends, family, and my staff—Tai Spence, Cerene Holley, Akera Brown, Brenda Mizell, Audrey

Harrison, Gina Harrison, Bill Kratz, Jennifer Gordon, Colleen Sullivan, Yael Milbert, Dejaniera B. Little, Kathy Williams, Kerry Ann Richards, Elaine Robinson, Rasheeda LaRue, Tisheba McCall, Jacelyn Boti, Joy Schneider and all the agents I have learned from and worked with over the years. I am grateful to Toby Salgado, owner of the Podcast *Superagentlive.com*, for his interview in 2016 that spearheaded my rise as a leader in the industry. My lead source, Alejandro DaVilla from *Landvoice.com,* who helped make my daily cold call grind 1000% more efficient. I am also extremely grateful to all my clients who have trusted me with the sale or purchase of their most valuable assets.

Lastly, I like to thank all the readers of this book. Thank you so much for your support. I hope my positive energy spills over into your dreams and goals, as you seek answers to how to become successful in Real Estate.

Deborah Spence

www.DeborahSpenceSoldIt.com

deborahspnc@yahoo.com

Chapter 1

My Story

IT WAS THREE DAYS AFTER CHRISTMAS, 2016, at approximately 10 am, when I left my last listing appointment of the year. It was cold and windy, and my nose was dripping from the onset of a cold. As I struggled to find a tissue in my oversized bag, I felt elated. It was a five-bedroom traditional home, priced at $200k in the City of Philadelphia. I was standing in the driveway next to my new Mercedes Benz, feeling like the happiest woman alive. I had achieved almost the impossible as a new real estate agent. I accomplished listing over 60 homes in my first year as a real estate agent…63 homes to be exact and sold 31 of them. I was as surprised as anyone, but also very proud of myself.

I had no magic formula for success. I learned a lot along the way. Most of which I can pass along to anyone who truly wants to embrace a new career path. Of course, the first step, and this should come as no surprise, is being ready to go all-in. This means hard work and plenty of hours, which is true for "making it" in any business. I worked hard at prospecting for new business twelve hours a day, seven days a week. You need to be ready, willing, and able to commit to such a vicious schedule.

But before I talk more about the How-to side of real estate, let me share with you some of my story. We learn a lot from our backgrounds, our experiences and our culture, some of which are lessons that will help us in our professional endeavors later in life.

I'm an African American woman, a single mother, and someone that suffers from a debilitating medical condition. I started out in very humbling conditions as the youngest of seven children born and raised in the brutal streets of the South Bronx, in New York City. My family survived only because of the kindness of charities such as the Catholic Church. They provided clothing, food, money and a discounted education to my family. I really appreciate the fact that with the help of the charities, and even some assistance from the government, my mom was able to raise all of us together. I saw many families divided because they were unable to provide for themselves or get the help they needed from elsewhere. I am grateful that we were not one of those families.

I knew early on that my life would be different. As I mentioned, I suffer from a debilitating medical condition. After the birth of my youngest child, I was diagnosed with paranoid schizophrenia, a mental illness that causes auditory hallucinations, which means hearing voices.

Initially, I could not believe my diagnosis and I was noncompliant with treatment. As I got older, and after having my second child, my condition worsened. As a result, my children were taken away, one went to live with his father and the other stayed with my mom.

I was placed involuntarily into several mental hospitals and wards. It took ten years of being in and out of hospitals for me to finally accept my condition and to find the best treatment plan. Although I'm much better today, I still take several medications each day and go for therapy to maintain my mental health. Unfortunately, although I'm doing well, it is a condition that I will suffer from for the rest of my life.

When I finally began getting better, I was able to restart my life. I moved from New York to Philadelphia to be with my partner. I was starting over emotionally and financially. I had several low paying part-time jobs, such as doing inventory early in the mornings in retail stores, temp work, light labor, and so on, just to make some money. The new relationship that I sought out in Philadelphia did not work out. I had a psychotic episode and was thrown out of the house. There I was homeless, underemployed, and broken emotionally. This was not the new start I had imagined. I vividly remember living in my car for six weeks before I was able to afford an apartment. My youngest son, who was not living with me, stayed with my ex-partner until I found the apartment. Then he moved in with me.

As tough as it was living in the South Bronx, living on the streets was an eye-opening and motivating experience for me. I read a lot of motivational books, most of which I will share in the appendix at the end of the book. I also read articles and blogs about my condition to learn different techniques to help minimize my symptoms. I became super-charged with changing my life and maintaining my health. I realized that I wanted a break from relationships and instead, I wanted to create a uniform routine to help me deal with the chaos in my mind.

At one point, I tried selling insurance in hopes of finding a career path. It didn't work out, but I knew something else was out there. It was just a matter of finding it. One of the most important things when it comes to changing your life is having a strong desire to make such a change—you must be totally open to doing it. I was open to finding something new and since I always wanted to go into business. The question now was; *how would I get there?*

Meanwhile, as I continued to improve my life, I learned my way around Philadelphia in a beaten-up old car, driving my son to all sorts of baseball and football games. He was always a good athlete, so when he wasn't in school, he was playing for some traveling team. It was good for me, since the more I drove him to games, the more I got to know the city. I liked Philadelphia more than New York because it was smaller and less complicated. Philadelphia has a lot of neighborhoods side by side, rather than the four very busy boroughs, and Staten Island, which I rarely ever visited.

At some point, while driving around my new founded home city I had some car troubles. I took my car to an auto repair shop to have a mechanic check it out. Never could I have guessed that a trip for auto repair would change my life. While the mechanic fixed my car, he talked about a vacant lot adjacent to the repair shop. He pointed out how one person might see the vacant lot as an eyesore, but how he saw millions of dollars in investment funds and a lucrative opportunity to develop an underdeveloped area. I didn't understand, so I kept asking questions. He explained that there was so much room for a developer to come and build, not just one house on this vacant lot, but someone could possibly build three houses and triple their investment. My mechanic explained that real estate was a great way for ordinary people to become financially independent and even wealthy. He wasn't wrong. When I researched real estate, I found many very successful real estate owners who knew how to buy and sell properties.

Despite my medical condition, I always had a *burning desire* to succeed and to take care of my family. I started pursuing real estate after having that conversation with my mechanic.

At the time, I was selling pre-paid cell phones for a local carrier. It was another in the long line of jobs I had after relocating to Philadelphia. I remember coming across an opportunity on Craigslist to become a manager of a popular pre-paid cell phone store. I went on an interview and was hired. After a few months, I had successfully turned around the sales of this small failing store and was then given an opportunity to move up to managing several stores in the area. I worked as a second level retailer under a master dealer, but sadly by the end of the month, after paying my expenses, I was not making any money. In fact, at the end of the month, I had to pay the master dealer to cover expenses that were not met from sales alone. This was very frustrating for me. It also didn't help that most of the people working for me did not want to work very hard. These were people with less ambition than the drug-dealers or con artists I saw in the South Bronx. In fact, they hated me because I was trying to work hard and make a living. They threatened to rob me, kidnap my family and other horrible things. They felt that I pushed them too hard because I expected them to show up each day on time and do some work. Many of them were annoyed that they were no longer eligible for public assistance. They blamed me, the manager, for all their problems. Meanwhile, I was getting more frustrated each month when I'd look at my bank account.

Finally, I recognized that this was a dead-end job. No money, no future, and people who wanted me dead. So, I thought about the conversation I'd had with my mechanic, with whom I'd developed a friendship, and it inspired me to go on the Internet to research real estate as a career. There are literally thousands of real estate sites, some good, some not so good, and some that are just a little bit strange. However, in the end, I realized that taking my career to the next level in sales, as a real estate agent, would be the best thing for me. I knew I had to take a risk. It was like jumping out of the window without a safety net, but I quit my managerial job and spent the next six weeks taking online classes for the real estate exam. I was so driven and so eager to start my career that I would stay up nights studying, reading, and learning everything about real estate law and real estate math. I remember one night when my son woke and went to use the bathroom, he looked at me and said, "Wow Mom, you're still studying? You make me want to go downstairs and read my textbooks." Of course, he didn't. He went right back to sleep.

My son's late-night comment, however, stuck in my mind. It illustrated how much he admired my determination. It was the impetus to keep me going. It had been years since I finished college, so my brain was a little foggy, and I still had some trouble with my hallucinations, which caused complications with my ability to comprehend and stay focused. But I was doing everything I could do to gain enough knowledge to pass the exam on my first attempt. As a result, and despite the odds, I passed the exam and became a licensed real estate agent.

I was quite overwhelmed at my accomplishment. The question now was; where do I begin? What company would be the best place for me to start my new career? I decided to go back online and search for local real estate agencies. I wanted to find a company that would allow me to maximize my commission. In addition, I wanted to work in a company that would provide the best training. So, I started working at Weichert Realtors, which is very well-known in the industry, especially as a good place for new agents. Unlike the cell phone business, the people were receptive and helpful. Like me, they wanted to build careers. Maybe real estate would be the answer. I knew the odds were still stacked against me, breaking into a new field, but I was ready to give it 100%.

∞ ∞ ∞

Burning Desire

Learning from Life Experiences

When I started at Weichert, I had no real sales experience. I had no one feeding me leads. I didn't know anyone in real estate sales and I didn't have any friends or family in the area in which I was currently licensed. But, what I did have was called 'street smarts.' These were lessons I had learned while growing up on the streets of the South Bronx.

Before relocating to Philadelphia, as I mentioned earlier, I lived in New York City's South Bronx. As a teenager, coming of age in the 1980s, I learned a lot about life from my environment. During the '80s, use of crack cocaine had become epidemic, poverty was at its worst in years, and the crime rate was very high. I was in the midst of drug dealers, gangs, con artists, hustlers, pimps, and gangsters which, I believed, spearheaded my early sales training.

For some reason, I didn't follow the wrong crowd or get into very bad habits. Instead, I liked to observe people. I remember watching a card game, called Three-card Monte, that con artists would play, mostly with tourists and out-of-towners. The goal of the game was for the participant to pick a playing card from the three the dealer shows him/her initially before playing. After the player selects a card, the dealer lays out all three cards, face down on a table or a board, shuffles them around and the player must then choose that very same initial card. It's the same concept you'll see on the scoreboards at most baseball games, where they hide a baseball under one of three caps and move them around quickly. You then need to pick the one the ball is under.

In the street version, there's gambling involved. The dealer bets small amounts at first, while pushing the player, very gently, to match the bets. The dealer, in the beginning, makes it very easy for the player to find the card. After a series of wins by the player, the dealer pretends to become frustrated at the player's ability to find the card. After several continuous losses, the dealer makes a final bet and says, "All or nothing." The dealer then puts down all the money that he or she supposedly has left. And now, entices the player to put down all the money that he or she has, including the winnings from the previous games. The player is pumped with excitement over outsmarting the dealer so much so that he or she agrees to put all his/her money in the pot. In many cases, this is hundreds, or even thousands, of dollars. So, guess who wins the final game? Yes, you are correct, the dealer. The player becomes shocked, angry, and embarrassed all within a matter of seconds, after realizing that this was a hustle. This may seem so obvious, but keep in mind, that a crowd usually forms around the players, which pumps up the excitement. Part of the crowd is comprised of the dealer's crew, while the rest are innocent bystanders, spectators amping up the player. As progress is seemingly made in the street game, the player is seen as a righteous savior battling all the wrongs of the world, to be played out on a street corner.

This "game" and the entire design and set up of the scam, along with all the other similar ones that I observed as a teenager, taught me a lot about sales techniques. No, I wasn't looking to trick people, but I was learning how to pique their interest and make them feel good on route to closing a sale. I learned the power of peer influence, crowd behavior, guiding your prospect into moving forward via self-discovery, learning when to walk away, transparency, talking less and listening more. But most importantly, what I enjoyed watching was how these street people convinced seemly normal average people to do things that they would not have ordinarily done on their own, by using their own brand of sales techniques.

My street education wasn't limited to Three-card Monte and other con games. I watched the drug dealers convince adults to try something that would help them get through their day with a little pick me up or figure out the right buttons to push to entice someone to buy the fashionable drugs of the day. I watched pimps convince beautiful girls, who could have their pick of any handsome law-abiding citizen, to sell their bodies and give the money to the pimp, all with the promise of his never-ending love and protection for them.

These were daily lessons about the weakness and vulnerability of the human mind. I had a front row seat to see how ordinary people threw out common sense for the promise of something that they felt was more important than their freedom. I was amazed and in awe. Not only did I unknowingly learn sales techniques, I also learned business skills from the streets in the Bronx. I watched how the "successful" drug dealers never used their own inventory, never worked the front of the "store," outsourced many menial tasks, promoted from within the ranks, rewarded loyalty, and so much more. There were also some locals who would dress in nice suits and take the early morning train downtown amid the 9 to 5ers, except they were not heading to an office to start their workday. Instead, they were going to steal stuff from one of the major department stores, bring the goods back to our neighborhood and sell the stolen merchandise in the evening to the people coming home from work. Many of whom were on the same trains with these "hustlers" that same morning. I would watch them present the merchandise, tell people it was the last one that they had (even though they had more in the car), and create a sense of urgency, "This is the last time you're going to see this—it's dirt cheap." You would hear the buzzwords and see how they would convince regular people to buy their goods. You could say, I got an early education, a business degree from the University of the South Bronx.

A Passion for Business

Two things I had in my favor when I started in real estate were passion and a drive to succeed. Some of that came from my personal struggles and some by learning so much while watching from the sidelines. By the time I was sixteen years old, I wanted to graduate from high school and go straight into the business world, become an entrepreneur, throw my hat in the ring. No, I did not want to be a con artist or hustle people. I knew where to draw the line. My street education taught me important business basics, not how to be a dealer or a hustler.

In fact, I went to a strict Catholic high school and it was so boring. I couldn't sit still and listen to the nuns talk on and on about how important it was to learn as much as you could, then graduate and get a good job, work there until you retire. It was dismal, so I often roamed the halls. One day, the dean became so tired of sending me to detention that instead she decided to sentence me to the guidance counselor's office. The guidance counselor told me that my punishment for that day was to pick a college out of this gigantic book and complete an application.

I picked Hofstra University because they had a business school and they had a scholarship program for inner city kids, like me, who scored high on the SATs. I took the SAT months earlier, only to practice my vocabulary. I had grown up around so many uneducated people (not necessarily bad people, just not formally educated), that my vocabulary was that of a grade-schooler or worse—a street hustler. If I was going to make it big as a businesswoman, I needed to learn how to speak correctly. Even today I'm still not 100% there. Partly because of improving my vocabulary, I was accepted into Hofstra University on a full scholarship. Unfortunately, I struggled to fit in during my years there and I also experienced early signs of my mental condition, which did not help my grades at all.

I did find solace in a family that I worked for as a daycare attendant. The Harrison family owned a home-based daycare center and they took a liking to me, especially Aunt Jean. She was the owner and operator, but all the kids, including myself, called her Aunt Jean even though her name was really Audrey. She was very kind, caring, and attentive to me, and welcomed me into her family during those early years while I was struggling in college. To this day we are still very close friends. I managed to graduate from Hofstra with a BA in Accounting and a minor in English, but my dreams of entrepreneurship died with my degree. My idealism was beaten out of me with textbook after textbook of memorization and robotic learning. Immediately after graduating from college, I had a baby boy and then seven years later I had my second son. By then my illness had become full blown.

Fast forward to today, my younger son is a teenager, still living with me. My older son, who's now 23, is living on his own in Philadelphia. We have a great relationship, which means so much to me. The years I did not have them with me were very difficult, but I needed to get the medical help that I received to become who I am today, not only as a successful business person but also as a mom.

While I did learn a lot from my days on the streets of the South Bronx, I do not advocate staking out neighborhoods that have drug problems and a significant amount of crime. I do, however, highly recommend that you think about what you have learned from your own life experiences that you can bring to a real estate career. I found some good in an otherwise difficult, life-situation and held onto the lessons I learned about human behavior. You'll hear many people tell you that they learned as much, if not more, about life in the real world than in the classroom or in textbooks. Don't underestimate the value of being observant. Take in what is going on around you. In an era in which people are often totally engaged in the sounds of their headsets or relentlessly staring at their iPhones, it's important to stop and look around for life lessons.

As I walked from my final sale of the year on that wintery day, to my fancy car, the cold didn't bother me in the least. I was finally basking in the warmth of success. I don't tell you this to brag, but to inspire anyone to follow my lead. If I could do this, anyone can.

Chapter 2

Finding Your Motivation: What's Your "Why?"

THERE ARE MANY POSITIVES TO starting a career as a residential real estate agent. For one thing, it gets you out of an office and into beautiful homes. You also have the flexibility to set your own schedule and make your own hours, which gives you opportunities to spend time with your family. In many ways, you are your own boss and there is no salary cap. The more you sell, the more you make. And if you are diligent, dedicated, and knowledgeable about the homes you are selling, you can do very well.

Sounds simple, doesn't it? Here's the catch. It's all up to you and how much you really, really want to succeed. You need to self-motivate and commit to working in a career that will require 12 to 14-hour days /seven days a week for the first three years. You need to push yourself even when you're tired or the weather isn't to your liking. You need to stay focused on your goals even when your iPhone is begging you to text with your friends, or a night of TV is just one click away on the remote. You need to have self-control and make the sacrifices to keep working hard toward your goal.

The question is why? Why would you do all of this?

I've heard people give several answers to this question. Some are tired of doing the same thing every day, making money for someone else. They want to get out and do something that is different from day to day. They want more control over their career paths. Others want to spend more time with their kids, go to their ball games, recitals, and class performances. Some like the idea of helping people make one of the biggest decisions in their life, buying a new home. Some want a part-time career, while others want a post-retirement career. For me the answer was simple: My "why?" was money. My sister died ten years ago, and I promised her, on her deathbed, that I would take care of her daughter and our mom. My mom never worked and was essentially unemployable. She didn't get her high school diploma and had no computer skills—not even the basics. My sister supported my mom and my niece financially. Her life insurance policy wouldn't last for the rest of their lives and I was running out of time. Even though my mom lived modestly, on only a few hundred dollars a month, the earnings from my sales job didn't even allow me to pay my own bills, and to take care of my boys. I had to do something to earn more. So, for me, real estate was the answer.

I saw real estate as a limitless opportunity, the more I sold the more I would make. After growing up and living in so much poverty, the idea of rising far above that was my burning desire. Once you dig down deep and find your burning desire, you will be able to use that as a motivating force. This need to succeed will become the one thing that keeps you up at night and energizes you in the morning.

Beyond knowing your "why?" and having a burning desire, you also need to have the following characteristics or skills:

- Determination, or drive;

- Focus and self-discipline;

- Organization;

- Commitment…a never quit attitude.

If you are determined, self-driven, focused, organized, and committed to the process, I assure you that you can go far. If these are not your strengths, you'll want to work on improving these attributes from the beginning.

With that in mind, let's take a closer look at some of the skills and characteristics mentioned above. Yes, you can hone these and other abilities. First, you need the determination to succeed, which comes from having a goal. If you examine your "why," (As in, 'Why real estate?') you can establish a goal, such as those mentioned above; having the freedom and flexibility in your career, controlling your destiny, making X amount of money annually, or perhaps all of these. You must then commit to reaching that goal. Determination (or drive) means how hard you then strive to reach that goal. It is your resolution to move forward despite any obstacles in your way. It is the strength of your character.

As for focus, I was laser focused on ultimately beating poverty and hopelessness and finding security, peace and happiness. Some people put photos in front of them as a constant reminder to stay focused. This might mean photos of the people who depend on you, such as your family. In my case, I posted the people I needed to take care of, my niece, my mom, and my boys.

On a practical note, focus means blocking out the excess, which is so important. Today, we have a ton of distractions vying for our attention all the time. I knew I needed to put every potential distraction aside if I was going to study and pass my real estate exams, so I used self-discipline to mentally block out everything I could (short of an emergency). I suggest putting a cage around everything that distracts you—mentally, of course. I wouldn't want you to cage up your family. Anyway, you get the gist of what I am saying. It doesn't mean you don't care about the people or things around you, it means you must prioritize and be able to put your career first as often as possible. This is the only way you can stay focused and motivated. It's the way entrepreneurs take a small business startup from their garage or basement and build a successful business. Remember, as a real estate agent you are also building your own business.

Organization can also be a huge factor in keeping you motivated. What helped me stay motivated was a whiteboard that my family had given to me for Christmas. On the top the board it simply said "Motivation." Now that is powerful, just staring at a blank whiteboard with motivation at the top. Along with the family photos I mentioned earlier, what became my super strength were the quotes I put on there, along with cards of inspiration that were sent to me, and, once I got it, I posted my real estate license on the board.

I also created a *morning routine*. It was easy for me to do because I already had a slightly different morning routine that I needed to do to manage my condition. I altered the routine with a different spin. The spin was to motivate myself to stay committed and to having a positive attitude, which I will talk more about a little later. Simple as it may sound, one way to create your positive attitude is to start your day with a consistent morning routine.

My *morning routine* starts when I wake up anywhere between 5 and 6 am. I start out by writing in my journal. I write my goals over and over again, my prayers, prayer list, thankful list, ideas, notes about life, quotes and even jokes. Then, I listen to an inspirational audiobook that I like for 20 minutes, write a "To Do" list, preview my calendar, review my goals, clean the house, iron my clothes, and check my bag, making sure I have all of the tools that I will need for the day (such as an electronic tape measure, both of my cell phones, my laptop, keys, notes, wallet, and on). Then I shower, brush my teeth, get dressed, and pray for a successful day.

A *morning routine* is something that you must set up right away. It will help you stay organized. But, most significantly, it will help you stay focused. After three weeks, it will become second nature, and you will follow that routine without even thinking about it.

Some people include things like exercise or yoga in their morning routine, as well as coffee and something to eat, even if it's a muffin. It's up to you, as long as it doesn't distract you from your goal of staying focused on your day ahead. It's also worth noting that if you are distracted by something nagging at you, write it down, or "park it" as they say, on a piece of paper or make a note on your phone, to deal with whatever it is at lunch or when you get home. The point is: you cannot get distracted. So, get it out of your mind and *onto* the paper or your cell phone. One other note is not to watch the news in the morning—it will serve as a distraction.

Now, you might be thinking, lots of people have routines, what does that have to do with real estate? Remember, you are not getting up and going to the office where your boss, or your administrative assistant, has everything mapped out for your day. You are your own boss *and* your administrative assistant. Real estate puts a lot on your shoulders, so a morning routine is so important since you have a lot of roles for which you need to prepare.

What about commitment? This is the toughest one. Consider how many people start a diet or join a gym and never commit to it. Why, because they don't see instant results. The same is true in selling real estate. People quit when they don't succeed immediately. In fact, it is estimated that 90% of salespeople quit after less than five rejections.

Can you commit? Yes, if your "why" is strong enough to keep you motivated at all times. Commitment means you will keep on going no matter what. If I had quit after three or four rejections, I have no idea what my life would be like today. I might still be in a dead-end job selling pre-paid cell phones.

It's important to remember that things don't happen all at once. Make a list of all the positives that you can get from staying the course. Look at the photos of the people who will benefit from your commitment and remind yourself of the benefits of this new direction in your life. But don't shoot for the stars all at once. I did not have "listing 60 homes," as a goal at the start of my first year. My motivation board said, "work hard, don't give up, and remember that hard work pays off." It was not until later in the year that I began to specifically write down my listing goal of 75 homes. I listed 63, so I came fairly close to my goal.

You might also keep in mind the inspirational words of Andrew Carnegie; *"Ninety percent of all millionaires become so through real estate."*

Burning Desire

∞ ∞ ∞

Educate Yourself

Blocking off time to do your initial research is essential as you want to know as much as possible before entering any industry. My secret to staying committed to my goal came from doing a lot of research and reading a lot of books. One book I read repeatedly was *No Excuses* by Brian Tracy. In his book, Tracy shares his life as a young man and his desire to make changes. He emphasized to the reader in plain and simple language, do not make excuses while pursuing your dream. His words were so encouraging that it added the extra fuel that I needed to stay the course, no matter how difficult it could become. I also read *Millionaire Real Estate Agent* by Gary Keller of Keller Williams Real Estate, and other industry books that helped me stay focused on becoming a real estate agent without a lot of experience.

Since real estate is a localized profession, and I knew I would be selling in one general area, I made a point of learning as much as I could about the areas in which I might be able to sell. I went out and drove around neighborhoods in Philadelphia to familiarize myself with possible territories. I also looked up the federal licensing exam requirements and the information for my state, which was, and still is, Pennsylvania. I went to the Pennsylvania Real Estate Commission website and they had a list of certified schools that can be used to take the classes. You will, in turn, need to research schools in your state and find courses you can take prior to taking the tests, local and federal. Also go online and learn all about the local housing market and join real estate groups on social media to get the inside scoop from people in the industry.

Get Organized

As I mentioned earlier, it is important to be well organized. It also helps to have good time management skills—actually, the two go hand in hand. Being well organized and managing your time effectively makes it easier to stay motivated because you won't have the disruption of constantly looking for the items you need or the frustration of being late for meetings or missing them altogether. Many rookie agents get frustrated and give up after six months, or less, in the business, not because of rejection, but because they have poor organizational and time management skills. They can't catch up with what they need to get done and, of course, they always think it's someone else's fault. Therefore, two other important rules of success are;

    1. Be accountable to yourself, and…

    2. Plan ahead.

Sure, there are situations that we cannot avoid, that can throw us off schedule or interfere with our plans, but the truth is that most of them arise because of a failure to plan ahead, organize your day and/or manage your time.

Remember, as your own boss, you can come and go as you please. No one tells you what to do, where to be, how to sell or how to manage your time. This sounds great and is one of the reasons why many people love real estate. It's great to be your own boss. But it can also become a problem. You need to know how to manage your time from the beginning. I read lots of books about time management and listened to several Audiobooks, as well. Look for books, apps, and articles on time management. Read them and take notes.

Get in the habit of using a calendar now, since it will become a vital tool for managing your time effectively. As you grow in your real estate career you'll have to allot more and more time to things that are really important, such as prospect calls, training, meeting clients and so forth. I keep a calendar and stick to my schedule. It's important as you get into the field, to organize your day in such a way that you will be available when the 9 to 5ers are also available. This means being ready for meetings before 9 am, after 5 pm, and on weekends. You will use your calendar a lot, whether it's on your phone, on another high-tech tool or it's something on which you simply write down your appointments.

The more you depend on your calendar, the more you will learn how to take control of your schedule and stick to it. Now, when a buyer calls and says we need to meet at 2 pm on Tuesday, I'll check my calendar to see if I'm available at that time or not. If not, I'll tell them that I'll have to meet them on another day—buyers have to go by my schedule. I cannot just run out the door at any time of day and put off the work I am scheduled to do. For example, I cannot focus only on buyers and shuffling them around all day long. If they decide not to buy, that's time *not* spent potentially earning money or prospecting for new clients.

You must have your schedule carefully planned out so that you are maximizing your time and you must try not to deviate from it often. You need to make out time to prospect for new business. You also cannot forget about training and sales meetings. I use the calendar on my phone which sends me an alert one hour before I prospect, one hour before I must take a buyer out, one hour before I have to meet a deadline, one hour before an appraisal. Managing your time and having the tools to help you are vital to your success, so I strongly suggest starting to use such tools ASAP.

∞ ∞ ∞

Write a Business Plan

I also suggest that you prepare a business plan. This is mostly for your own purposes, but you can use it when going on interviews for jobs. Just as entrepreneurs use business plans to show lenders and investors that they are prepared to take on the challenges of owning a business, you are ready to take on your own real estate business. A business plan should have your goals on it and an action plan for meeting those goals. For example, it might say; set up an Open House every weekend, cold call expired listings or "for sale by owners" listings, door knocking, flyer distributions, seminars, networking events, social media, blogging, and so on. It will also include a marketing plan. How do you plan to spread the word that you have listings to sell?

The more you learn on your own and in school, prior to taking your real estate classes, the easier it will be to prepare a business plan.

You should also have an idea of how much you can earn and what it will take to reach a number that you can set up as your goal. You can then start punching up some numbers. I came up with the number 75 homes listed by using a business plan my company had given new agents. I calculated that if I listed 75 homes and if 80% sold I would have a gross commission of well over six figures. You might choose to be more conservative and estimate selling 50% of your listings, which was what I ended up selling in my first year (I sold 31 of 63 listed or 49%). Set a goal for yourself and see what it will take to reach it. Research the average cost of a home in your area and then, calculate the average sales commission, so you can get an idea of what you can earn. For example, if the average home sells in your projected sales territory for $200,000 and you get a 6% commission that would be $12,000 which is split between the agents for the buyer and the seller, giving you $6,000. If you listed 50 homes and sold 25, you would make $6,000 x 25 or $150,000 less marketing fees, a fall through at a 10% rate (this is when an agreement is terminated because of inspection issues, mortgage issues, or emergencies) and other dues. Even if all these additional fees come to 15%, or in this case $22,500 you will have $127,500 profit, topping your goal of $100,000. The point is, work the numbers and add them to your business plan.

Value Each and Every Accomplishment

If you are a parent, you can relate to the impact of small accomplishments. When your baby takes their first steps or says their first words, you are so excited. Then, when they do well on a test in school, make it onto a team or land a role in the school play; again, you are excited for them. This is how you should approach life in general, appreciating and valuing the little accomplishments along the way. Sometimes we tend to gloss over them, focusing on the results down the road instead. The problem is, if you look too far ahead, you can lose sight of the many small accomplishments it takes to reach your ultimate goal. This is why so many people quit before they get started- they don't want to put in the effort (and take the small steps) to get to where they want to go. That's why I say; value each accomplishment along the way. These are the steps it takes to succeed. Celebrate those steps. Appreciate them.

Every accomplishment I made, even the small ones, was listed on my motivational board. When I signed up to take my real estate exam it went on the board, and when I passed it, that went on the board in big letters. Even if it was something really small (like listing an appointment) I would put it on the motivational board to show I was making progress. By listing accomplishments, little by little along the way, you will show yourself that you are making progress. Remember, slow and steady wins the race. It was those little things that I put up on the board that kept me motivated and encouraged me. They still motivate me every day.

I remember posting my first listing; it came from a cold call. I started out the first weekday after getting licensed. I remember it was the first Monday after the Thanksgiving of 2015. I went through the For Sale by Owner listings on Craigslist. I was making calls from the list and I spoke to a gentleman who had a house to sell in South Philadelphia. I went over my sales pitch, which I pulled from Google, and he agreed to meet with me.

I remember meeting him, and his wife. I did my prepared presentation, but he wasn't sure if he wanted to pay a commission. He started going on and on and on with all these reasons why he didn't want to work with an agent. So, I asked his wife; do you really want strangers from Craigslist just randomly coming to your home? She said "No," and asked, "where do we sign?" In the end, it was his wife who decided to move forward.

I remember putting my first listing up on the board. Each step of the way, I posted my accomplishments. It's a good way to monitor progress, and it works (not only in real estate but in anything you're trying to accomplish in life). Recognize the importance of each accomplishment along the way, like you did when your son or daughter took their first steps, said their first words or made their first drawings, which you posted on the refrigerator.

Be Prepared

If you're prepared, you will build the self-confidence necessary to put you on top of your game. As I mentioned above, I started making cold calls to get listings, with my first prepared speech coming from Google.

It's hard to prepare for cold calling, but you need to do so. You need to adopt a mindset that you are not going to take anything anyone says personally. If you don't do this, you will never survive cold calling.

First, make sure you are setting yourself up to succeed. Your call list should only comprise people looking to sell their homes. This way you are speaking to the right demographic group. Also try calling at optimal times, not too early, not too late, and not on major holidays, or during the Super Bowl. Next, you need to be confident and work from a script (but try not to sound scripted). Know your sales pitch, which should include what you can do for them, (people always want to know 'what's in it for me?"). Let them know why it benefits them to work with you. Also, take nothing they say personally. I repeat; take nothing they say personally! They don't know you, so if they are rude, crude, nasty or totally obnoxious it has nothing to do with you. Cold calling is fraught with rejection, that's part of the job. Estimate that only one out of ten people will talk with you and only some of those will list with you.

The more calls I made, the easier it became to create my own sales pitch which began by announcing who I was, mentioning my company and explaining that I was looking to help them sell their home. After that, if they were interested, it turned into a conversation and I would listen and ask them why they wanted to sell. Once they realized it was an actual person on the phone and not a robotic call, people would talk about their home and the conversation would go off script. In time, it became easier for me keep the conversation going. I was shy, so this was a major challenge for me. But, the more conversations I had the more confident I became. I would talk about real estate and they would talk about their homes and what they are looking to accomplish. By having them talk more, I could find out from the prospect why are they selling, and what was the motivation. Finding out why they want to sell is a good thing, because you can always go back to that. The sales process has its ups and downs, people may put in an offer and then rescind the offer, or the house may not pass inspection, and so forth. When things like this happen, you can go back to the sellers and remind them why they are selling, Even after they agree to meet with you, or you get them to agree to let you sell their property, you can remind them of their goal, to reduce stress in their life, to downsize to something smaller, or the need for something larger; whatever it is that keeps them going. This is their "why?" as in "Why they are selling." The more you get them to talk about their motivation to sell, the easier it is to keep the process going.

One couple wanted to sell before their granddaughter was born. They would then use the money to spoil their granddaughter. In this case, when the couple started getting frustrated with the process, I reminded them about the opportunity to spoil their soon-to-be granddaughter. This kept them motivated to sell. In the end, the house sold, and the day of the closing was the day their daughter went into labor. And yes, it made it onto my motivation board.

I also knew how important it was for me to be prepared for meetings. When I first met the people who later gave me my first listing, I was very nervous, so I made sure to get there early. In fact, I was about an hour early, so I pulled into a nearby McDonald's parking lot and sat and prayed for the energy, the strength, and the wisdom—everything I could think of. I wanted to say the right things, and I wanted to be cool and calm. They didn't know it was my first appointment. I went over what I was going to say and remembered what we talked about on the phone call (always, always take notes!).

Being there early and having time to get myself together became a ritual of mine. And you should make it part of your routine. I did it again, for every listing appointment I got. I would get there about 15 to 20 minutes in advance of the appointment and I'd sit in the car and calm my nerves and reduce my anxiety. I also started doing a lot of visualization. I would visualize them saying 'yes,' signing the documents, and so on. By arriving early, I was able to get myself into selling mode and out of shy person mode. This is difficult if you are an introvert. I have to talk myself into it all the time.

Being early and having the time to prepare, and motivate yourself, makes a world of difference. If you are running late, you will become very anxious and you won't have the time for the all-important preparation and self-motivation.

∞ ∞ ∞

Stay Committed

When we decide to commit to a goal or a dream, often we fall short because we focus on the wrong things or let the negatives take over. It's very easy to make up excuses and find reasons why it will not work instead. People often use the following excuses;

- I'll never make any money in this field.

- No one will want to take a chance on me.

- I'm not really a salesperson.

- I can't take the rejection.

- I'm not cut out to do this.

There are so many excuses available, that I could easily fill a chapter with them. But I won't because I do not believe in making excuses. I realized right away that I made the right decision, but after three months, with paychecks not showing up too quickly, I started second guessing myself. I thought maybe this isn't right for me, maybe I'm better off with a weekly paycheck. Then I realized that my weekly paycheck was not getting me anywhere. There's a saying, "if you want something done right, you need to do it yourself." This meant that if I wanted to make more money, I'd have to take matters into my own hands. So, I moved forward, realizing that in real estate, like starting any business, you must make sacrifices and overcome challenges to make something big happen.

Staying committed to my goal was one of the hardest things I ever had to do, but I am so proud, and you will be too, when you accomplish listing 50 or 60 homes in one year. The commitment that I had to achieving my listings goal also carried over to the other goals that I had at the time; I lost weight, became a better listener, and became a great communicator. I was not born with these character traits. As I mentioned, I am naturally an extremely shy person, an introvert, and I don't feel comfortable at all in social settings. I pushed forward and reached my goals, and as I also said before, if I could do it coming from my background, so can you. The catch is that you must put in the time and effort.

And finally, I know that many people fail because they are filled with excuses and lies. People will read these pages and tell themselves over and over again that Deborah Spence was lucky, she just had good timing, and she entered real estate during a good market. It's not possible to be successful in one year, or two or even three. I can't; because I can't; because I can't, I can't, I can't!

Well, I want you to do one very important thing for me, please. I want you to give up the word "can't," remove it from your vocabulary. Write it down again and again on paper and throw the paper out, until you have had enough of the word. I do not use the word at all about anything that I want to do in my life. I did not say I can't be a real estate agent because I was a poor woman with no sales experience. And I did not even remember those words when Weichert Top Management acknowledged me at their annual golf/managers meeting and all 140 managers gave me a standing ovation for my success. I do not use those words when I do speaking engagement today and I did not use them when I decided to sit down and write this book. I just went on and did all the above with the desire, energy and excitement as if I had already accomplished it all.

You can do it, too! Start with small steps and small accomplishments, and keep moving forward. Remember the popular saying, "the journey of a thousand miles begins with one step," or to paraphrase, *listing 40, 50 or 60 homes, begins by listing one.*

Chapter 3:

Finding a Home in Real Estate: Where Will You Work?

CONVERSATION WITH MY MECHANIC – who would have thought the guy who knew all about cars, would set me on a career path to selling houses? But, as I mentioned earlier, that's exactly how it happened. It not only started me on a path to learning as much as I could about real estate, but I started thinking about where I was at the time, making hardly any money in a dead-end job, and how much I needed a job that I had control over, something in which I could grow and earn a lot more money.

In this chapter, I want to fill you in on the path you will follow once you have passed the real estate exams in your state. You will have to meet the criteria which may include a criminal background check, being a resident of the state, high school graduate and legal age—some states 18, others 19. There are also application fees in each state plus continuing education courses required, which differ from state to state. In Pennsylvania, for example, you will need 14 hours of Pennsylvania Real Estate Commissions approved continuing education during every two-year renewal cycle of your license. But keeping yourself educated is a lot more than just doing the necessary hours, it's about keeping you up on the latest changes in the real estate market, and there are plenty of them. You need to know this stuff. Education doesn't end when you finish studying for, and passing, your real estate license exams. It increases. And if real estate becomes your passion (and it should if you're going to succeed), you will actually enjoy learning more about the industry. I love it.

One place to find out a lot about real estate, including requirements and courses, is the National Association of Realtors® (NAR), which has over one million members all throughout the country and promotes the most effective government regulations. All members must follow a standard code of ethics. The NAR is also the organization that holds the trademark on the title REALTOR®, which can only be used by paid members. As a member, I enjoy the benefits of having support from the organization, free access to all the forms that we use, plus technical support, and advocacy. This is something you should add to your motivation list—join the NAR and become a REALTOR®.

Where to Work?

DEBORAH ANN SPENCE

And now it's time to find a home, no, not for a buyer, for you—a real estate agency you can call home. You'll want to carefully select where you want to work. It's an important decision. Of course, it's not up to you alone, real estate firms will want to know what you are bringing to the table before accepting you into their real estate firm.

First, let's talk about selecting the company that you would like to work for. Here are ten things to consider:

- What are the fees that you will be required to pay?
- How much is your commission split?
- Are you being paid a salary or straight commission?
- Is there opportunity for growth?
- Will you fit in with the office culture?
- Does the company have a good reputation?
- Is the company independent or franchised?
- Is the company private or a public corporation?
- Will you be independent or part of a team?
- Does the company offer training?

You need to know the answers to all the above questions before parking your license with a broker. As a new agent, you are required to work under supervision of an experienced broker for two or three years, depending on your state rules. This means you work at a firm, have your freedom, but are under the watchful eye of a broker, who handles your commissions and makes sure you comply with state and company rules.

Some companies pay all their agents a 100% commission; however, you must pay monthly desk fees, coaching fees, copier fees, errors and omission fees, and transaction fees. Most companies, however, like Weichert, start new agents at a base commission of 50/50 or 60/40 initially until they become experienced producers. When working for a company that pays a commission split, you normally have minimal fees, such as MLS dues, Board of Realtor® dues, and errors and omission fees. A lot of new agents focus heavily on commission splits, but there are other factors involved. You need to think back on the goals you set for yourself in this business. If, for example, you are looking for a part time job or simply do not have the time or the personality to prospect for hours and hours, there are discount or transactional companies that pay new agents a salary. Agents are paid to show homes. However, if there is a sale, a more experienced agent completes the transaction. For part timers who are unable to prospect for work, but want some income, this can work out well.

Some companies give new agents the opportunity to grow quickly into management roles and other leadership positions. There are companies that attract younger agents because they have an office culture that may be more casual. The dress code may be casual, and the office space may be designed for creative thinking and brainstorming, but agents still need to produce. There are also companies with a more conservative, old-school, culture. Decide what works best for you.

Reputation in the real estate industry is everything. It is important to carefully research the companies that interest you, as well as the broker, before parking your license. There is also a difference between a private real estate company and a public real estate company. In my opinion, public companies focus on driving sales and spend a lot of time recruiting new agents to drive up the numbers. Private companies are more focused on branding and individual agent development as opposed to being sales driven. *Keep in mind that this is only my opinion and I recommend that you do your own research and interview with a lot of companies before moving forward.*

Some new agents may feel more comfortable working with a team of agents as opposed to doing it alone. There are both benefits and drawbacks to joining a team. Some have lower commission splits but make up for it with experienced team leaders who can help you learn the business quickly, through coaching and mentoring. Many people find that they learn a lot more by finding a mentor.

Then there are the expenses, both office and personal. These will vary depending where you choose as your home base. The company may do advertising and give you a piece of that ad space, or you may need to do all your marketing on your own. You may work from their offices or from home on your own phone. Ask the questions, then do some math and keep in mind what you can and cannot deduct, depending on the latest tax laws. Again, the more expenses you must pay, the higher the commission you may receive. Typically, it's a trade off. The more the real estate company does to help you, the lower the commission split. And conversely, the more you are out there on your own, the higher the commission split. But, as mentioned earlier, it's not just about the split. We all need some training, some people more than others.

Expenses have changed a bit over the years. Today, they are handled in more of a "co-op" (or shared) manner than in the past. In the old days you had to pay a desk fee, which meant you were essentially renting desk space. Now companies estimate how many agents they will need to cover the expenses of the office, which will include things like; copiers, phone bills, secretaries, Wi-Fi, computers, software programs, etc. Let's say they have $10,000 of expenses per month and they divide that by 50 agents. In that case each agent would pay $200 each month in expenses or, if they have 100 agents, they would pay $100 a month. Along with paying office expenses, companies offer additional features. For example, at my company, anyone can use the copier or fax machine for an unlimited amount of time, plus we have a conference room and a receptionist. Some companies have you chip in more because they are in high end areas and need to make the right impression. Other companies charge lower expenses, but then have you pay extra for a lot of the little things, like copies. It all depends on the company you choose. Keep in mind that higher commission splits may be offset by higher expenses, so take everything into consideration.

DEBORAH ANN SPENCE

I must say that as a new agent with no money coming in, it can be difficult to start out from day one having to pay $100 or $200 each month. I remember that I quit my previous job in August and started in real estate in November. By that time, I had spent whatever I had left over for living expenses. I had no money and no option but to work hard to make money fast. It took me only six weeks to get a commission check, but it can take new agents six months, or longer. My partner covered me financially for a few months in-between. You will likely need some help getting by until the first commission checks start coming in. Retirees may have a pension or 401k to cover them while other new agents may take part-time work with another job at night.

The good thing about this field, and very motivating, is that rather than a typical job in which there are few decisions, you have various possible scenarios as presented by the real estate companies. Remember, you are an independent contractor, and there is some flexibility…but you still need to be asked to work for a certain company. They need to feel comfortable about bringing you on board. In some cases, a team leader, or a company in general, will expect you to have your own lead base to bring to the table, in other cases they will provide leads, but your commission split will be lower. I was looking for a situation in which a new agent could feel comfortable and get training and support. Yet, I still wanted my freedom and the ability to get down and prospect like crazy.

When I started Interviewing with companies I was not at all prepared. I was like; "I've got my license, I'm excited, now what's the next step?" They asked me who I knew. Do you know people that have a home and are looking to sell? Do you know people looking to purchase a home? Do you have a large sphere of influence? I must admit, I wasn't even totally sure what that meant at the time. Don't worry, I'll discuss it later. They asked if I belonged to organizations, community groups and so forth. Clearly, I was unprepared and the first real estate agencies I visited could see that I was naïve, and they rejected me. Fortunately, Weichert recognized my enthusiasm and must have seen that I was very determined. They hired me, and I was excited because they were great at training new agents. Different agencies will be the right fit for different people.

Today, if I was looking for a real estate company, I'd have a business plan. It might only be one page, but it would include my sphere of influence—not name by name, but things like the organizations I belong to, types of people I know in the community, homeowners I know, my social media following, etc. Basically, some sphere of influence to show that I have a plan for who I'd call first. I'd also include ways in which I would market listings—from open houses to ad placement, and to any other ideas that would spread the word in the areas in which I might be selling homes. I'd also demonstrate that I know a lot about the local real estate market. When you discuss the industry, include books that you've read and the classes or seminars you've attended on your business plan (and/or resume), they see that you've done your homework and that you are committed to being part of the industry.

Research helps you learn about the different real estate companies. You can search the internet and find out all sorts of things, like which companies have the highest market share in your area. For me, it meant looking for companies in Jenkintown or Philadelphia. I looked up the top ten real estate companies in the area on sites like Realtor.com®, Zillow.com, and Trulia.com.

Once the selection of where you will work is over, (meaning they've invited you to work with them) the question is what do I do next? There are two answers:

1. Prepare;
2. Prospect All Day Long.

∞ ∞ ∞

A Little Preparation Goes a Long Way

Okay, you've found a real estate agency to call home. Now what? First, you'll need a lot of business cards. Many real estate firms will supply you with cards. When I started out they gave me about 1,000 business cards to get started. If I didn't have cards, I would have grabbed a chunk of my manager's cards and tell people that I'm on his team.

Alas, you will need to determine your Sphere of Influence (SOI). No, it is not something out of Star Trek. Your Sphere of Influence is made up of the people that you know who can help you get your new business off the ground with leads and referrals. It starts with the people closest to you, such as your friends, neighbors and relatives. Then it expands from there. Your SOI includes previous business associates, people at your gym, on your bowling team, in your old car pool, parents of your son or daughter's teammates on their soccer team, little league team, or in their karate classes, school choir, Boy Scouts or Girls Scout's troop. Let's not forget your doctor, dentist, chiropractor, the vet who takes care of your dog or cat, your accountant, attorney, financial advisor, psychologist, psychic or spiritual leader. Include anyone you have done business with, such as contractors or vendors as well as people you know from local organizations, church groups, clubs, volunteer organizations, the local PTA, or the Chamber of Commerce.

You may also know people who are already connected with the real estate industry such as; a building manager, home inspector, title agent, relocation manager, property manager, commercial real estate agent, mortgage professional, developer, architect, out of state agent, engineer, interior designer or even another real estate agent working in another territory. Don't forget your landlord and/or your neighbors. The point is, there are a lot more people in your life than you think. Just start making a list and keep expanding it as you meet more people. You never know where a referral will come from. Remember, I started in real estate because of a conversation with my mechanic—so add your mechanic to your SOI list. And keep in mind that it is not about just the 100 or 200 people on your list, it's also about the people in their spheres of influence. Let them help you market your services to the people they know.

Make sure to use a good software program to maintain your listings, such as a Customer Relationship Management system (CRM) and refer to it often, and back up whatever you are using for your list in the cloud or someplace else that is not on your computer. Protect the names of contacts on your list(s). You have a lot riding on them. And never give them out to anyone!!

Let me also add one of the most obvious ways of building up your list—social media. The big positive of the social media is that you can spread the word far and wide, which is why they call it the World Wide Web. However, you need to look for local people, so you must be careful not to waste time with people far from your areas of business. So, if you're working with sellers in the suburbs of Chicago, and someone from Tibet wants you to sell his house, you'll want to get off the phone quickly. While social media is helpful, it can take some time to build and establish relationships in, or around, your geographic region. I have made sales thanks to online relationships, but it took about a year of establishing myself and letting people get to know and trust me before it worked. You need to let people know that you are knowledgeable about the industry by answering questions, participating in groups and posting informative material.

Of course, if you typically use social media to connect with people who are already in your SOI, jump right in and let them know what you are up to and ask them to please let you know if they are looking to buy or sell their home soon or if they could recommend you to other people that they know. Don't forget to thank them and leave your contact info, even if you think they already have it. This may sound obvious, but remember…when someone contacts you, get back to them quickly. Also, realize that people may have no immediate need for your services right now, but you may get contacted by a referral six months, or even a year, later.

I also suggest that very early on, you arrange a "Meet and Greet," cocktail party and invite up to 50 people in your sphere of influence. This is your "coming out" party as a real estate agent, so make it a fun event and try to spend time talking to each and every person in the room. Tell them what you are trying to accomplish and ask them for a little help. People who like you and want you to succeed are usually very happy to assist you if they can. The party will hopefully help you generate a list of 100 names and numbers for you to call.

Since I had relocated from another state, I had no family or friends nearby to call on for help. Therefore, I was on my own. In such a situation you will need to buckle down and make a lot of cold calls to generate your own leads. If you don't have a big sphere of influence, get out and join local groups, associations and get involved in your community. Look for networking groups in your area and attend some get-togethers(remembering to always have your business cards with you). Rumor has it that there are agents who have been pulled over by the cops and not only handed the officer their license and registration but also included a business card.

Utilizing your sphere of Influence is great, but you will still need to reach out farther, if you want to make real money and enjoy success. You'll want to contact recently expired listings, old expired listings and for sale by owner (FSBO) listings. How do you do that? I'll tell you. Your agency should have access to such listings. But it is up to you to pick up the phone and make cold calls. Do not drop to the floor in distress. To accelerate your success without having someone spoon-feeding you leads or having to spend thousands of dollars each month on internet advertisement, you need to pick up the phone and make cold calls. That is exactly what I did on day one at my office. I started making cold calls to expired listings and for sale by owners (FSBO) listings.

Prospecting

First, before reaching out to people outside of your SOI, remember your goals and your burning ringing desire to succeed. I say this because once you start calling people that you do not already know; you need to be prepared to speak to some nasty, angry, arrogant, horrible people. Yes, they are out there, and no, they should not have any impact on your day, your job or anything else. Some of these folks may just be having a bad day, while others are just unpleasant for their own reasons. In some cases, people are angry at the world. Conversely, you will also get people who are lonely and just want to chat. You need to "nicely" move along if you do not think this person has any interest in listing, or buying, a house. Make sure that before you start calling, you have a speech prepared, such as the ones I include below.

You want to let them know who you are, where you are from, and that you can help them list and sell their home. If they are still with you, then you can shift to your presentation, or sales pitch, which is basically what you can do that will help them sell their homes quickly and get a fair price.

I explain that I have a list of the websites that we use to post the listings, such as realtor.com®, and zillow.com. I also tell the seller about our unique 800 number. We are the only company that has this kind of 800 number that has calls patched to an agent in three minutes to schedule an appointment for the buyers to see the house. So, if a call comes through that is for one of my listings, I'll get it within three minutes and be able to set up an appointment with potential buyers.

I also explain the Open House program where we have an Open House every weekend until the home sells. To spread the word about the Open House, we put out eight to ten directional signs plus lots of balloons and have food available when folks show up. In addition, we call about 100 neighbors and invite them over in case they know someone who may be looking to buy or sell. Plus, they can also see how we do an open house in the event they are looking to sell their homes.

If sellers start talking about selling their home on the phone call, I talk about the real estate market in their area and I can also answer the most important question: How much can we get for it? If they describe the home, I can give them the going price for similar houses in the area, just as a baseline. So, for example, if they tell me it's a single, detached home, with three bedrooms and two bathrooms on Such & Such Street, I can look at a list of similar houses in that area and see that a similar house sold recently for $350,000. I also let them know that I can come over tomorrow, see the house, and give them a more specific estimate.

Remember, all the above is under the assumption that people are interested in talking to you. Many people will not be ready to converse. The key to phone calls and prospecting is to remain positive and realize that the more rejections you get, the closer you are to getting a listing and making a sale. Olympic skier Shaun White used to say that the more times he fell in practice, the better. He explained that by getting all the falls out of the way early on, he was then more likely to have a great run when he competed. In other words, once you get the failures out of the way, you'll be closer to success! Therefore, all those negative responses mean a positive one is coming up.

What about Experience?

When you're new to an industry—or a job in general—you typically do not have a lot of experience. So how do you handle that?

As a new real estate agent, I used the experience of my company and the other agents in my office as a way of providing the experience necessary for a seller to hire me. I would say that "my company," just sold a home in your area for top dollar or that "my company" just listed a home in your area. By calling around to the just listed and just sold contacts provided proof to the seller that the company is very active and successful in the neighborhood. When you are new in the business you need a "brag list" of things to say, a list of your accomplishments. Since you don't have such a list yet, let the success of the company speak for you—that's where you get your initial "brag list."

I've had good luck going through expired listings, where sellers had their homes up for sale recently, but for whatever reason, it did not sell. In these situations, the contract that the seller had with their agent has since expired. If the agent is unable to get them to re-sign a new agreement, then you have free range to cold call, knock on their doors, and pursue them for business. Here is the script that I use when cold calling people whose listings have expired.

"Hello. my name is Deborah Spence, from Weichert Realtors. I noticed your home was taken off the market and my manager told me to reach out to you to see if I

can help you get it back on the market and sold quickly. Are you available today or tomorrow for me to stop by for 10 minutes to share my re-marketing strategy with you?" This is a strategy that was named by one of the managers at my company, which is essentially re-evaluating the market and making a new marketing plan, or a "re-marketing plan," as he called it.

Then there are the FSBOs, the sellers who'd rather sell their home on their own. Typically, they have had bad experiences with a real estate agent in the past or they simply may not want to pay commission. Often, they are so emotionally attached to the home that they feel they would be the best person to convince a potential buyer to purchase the home. The sellers may be scared that if they hand over the listing and the job of selling the house that they are giving up their role in the process. I try to alleviate those fears. I always show my professionalism by creating flexibility in the contract as well as including them in the sales process. I let them know that I am helping them through the process of selling their home, not taking the process away from them or taking control of their house. I want them to understand that as a professional, I can make objective selling points based on my knowledge of the homes in the neighborhood and how the home measures up to other homebuyers will look at in the area. As a result, I've had a lot of success selling homes listed initially as FSBOs.

Burning Desire

Here is the script *I use* when calling FSBO's on the phone:

"Hello, my name is Deborah Spence, from Weichert Realtors. I'm local in the area and I noticed that you are selling your home for sale by owner. I hope you have the best of luck selling on your own, however, if at some point, you get frustrated with the process, I would love to be at the top of the list of Realtors® you interview. Would it be okay, if I stopped by today or tomorrow, briefly, to take a look at your beautiful home and maybe if you have extra time, I could share with you my marketing strategy and take measurements, so you can get your home sold quickly."

I also cold call neighbors of homes that agents in my office just listed or homes that I just listed. My intentions are to tell the neighbors that I just sold a home in their neighborhood and that I am a local real estate agent. This is my opportunity to introduce myself in case they also might be interested in selling.

This is my simple script for these calls:

"Hello, my name is Deborah Spence and I am with Weichert Realtors. I am calling to let you know that I (or an agent in my office) just sold a home in your neighborhood and received top dollar. Are you interested in knowing the value of your home or are you interested in selling as well? I can stop by today or tomorrow and share my ideas with you.

After I was hired by Weichert Realtor's assistant manager, I began work right away. I arrived at the office at 7am and spent eight hours calling FSBOs. I was able to generate an appointment that very first day. I did it because I had that burning desire to succeed as mentioned earlier.

Remember, you are working within a company, but it is all up to you to motivate yourself and use the listings you get in the office, and external leads from your SOI. Of course, without a boss hovering around you making sure you do your job, make your calls and get leads, you have the responsibility of holding yourself accountable. I still hold myself accountable because if I don't do it, who will? I even punish myself if I do not put in the number of hours I need. Punishment includes: double cold call hours the next day, door knocking for an hour the next day in the cold, snow, rain or heat, staying later in the office, coming in an hour earlier the next day, doing two open houses on the weekend instead of one, or a four-hour Open House on the weekend instead of a more typical two hour. In other words, I make myself work twice as hard for the time I was slacking off. This is because failure was not, and is not, an option. It all goes back to your drive and those photos on your motivation board. Too many people are afraid of hard work and holding themselves accountable. But if you talk with successful people, almost all of them have had to work hard, the others just got lucky, and you cannot at any rate and for any reason, count on luck!

House Tours

One of the best parts of being a real estate agent is getting to see all sorts of terrific houses. To appropriately list a house, and sell a house, you must see the house. When people take you through their homes they will tell you all sorts of great things. They will tell you about some of the things they have done to update and modernize the house, along with personal stories, family stories, and even the great history of the house..." Did you know that George Washington slept here?" That can be quite interesting when it comes from a seller whose house was built in 1922. Yes, people love their homes, and some tend to exaggerate a bit, but you need to pay close attention to what you are looking at.

When you walk around you want to see what has been done to the house and what needs to be done. If, for example, you know that three-bedroom, two-bathroom houses in a certain area have averaged selling for $350,000, you can use that as a general starting point and raise or lower the asking price based on what you see.

For example, you can see if the kitchen is updated and whether the bathroom(s) have been remodeled. Keep in mind that kitchens and bathrooms sell houses. A new kitchen could raise the asking price by $25,000, a new bathroom, perhaps $10,000. Conversely, an older kitchen that needs to be updated could drop the price by $25,000 and a bathroom by $10,000. In other rooms, you might see torn carpeting, which could drop the listing by $5,000, and so on. Hardwood floors, ceiling fans, central air, a porch, a sunroom, an addition to the house are all plusses. Wear and tear and rooms in need of repair are minuses. Other factors that can lower the asking price might include poor plumbing, roofing issues, or an old furnish that needs to be replaced. On the flip side, curb appeal helps, fresh paint, new windows, a well-manicured lawn, etc., can add value. While you can't do anything about a bright purple house across the street, sellers can, if they choose to, make a lot of improvements to raise the value of the house. You also need to know what's popular in certain areas. For example, in a city, a rooftop deck may be all the rage, while in a suburban neighborhood, a landscaped yard, a large deck, and a finished basement, might be what people are looking for. You will learn early on what the latest "must haves" are in your areas of business.

Once we finish the tour, I then take control and ask the sellers to sit down with me at the kitchen table, so we can have a discussion. I tell them that a lot of buyers in this market want move-in ready homes with up to date kitchens and bathrooms and ask if they are planning to update the home by making some of the necessary changes. Some will say, "just sell it as is" since I won't be living here." This will lower the value, which is fine with these sellers. Others will say they will upgrade the house to raise the value.

You will then be able to come up with a fair asking price, provided the sellers do what they say they will do. If they are selling it "as is," which may be considered "a fixer-upper," you can get to work right away. The point is, by gathering your information, you will be able to provide a pretty accurate answer for the ever-popular question; how much I can get for it?"

Once you have taken the tour, gotten to know the sellers, and their house, fairly well, it will be time to do the ever popular "Open House," which I will discuss in the next chapter.

Chapter 4

Marketing, Open Houses and Buyers

NCE YOU'VE ENTERED THE WORLD OF real estate as a licensed agent, you'll find that along with sellers, listings and sales, you'll need to master the art of marketing, hold awesome open houses and get the gist of working with buyers.

When I realized that just getting listings would not put money in my pocket, I began learning about marketing and how to increase activity for the seller's home. Once again, as a reader, I read articles on the internet and reviewed some real estate books. I learned that to generate more action for the home to sell, I would need to do the following...and so will you:

DEBORAH ANN SPENCE

1. *Use Social Media Often.* The key to social media success is getting your friends and family to help you become successful in real estate. When you post your new listings on Facebook, Instagram, Google+, Pinterest, etc., the goal is for your friends to share new listings and Open House invitations with their friends. Also, when using social media, you will meet new people, but the relationship has to become a two-way street. You must engage and join conversations, "like" people's comments and photos, as well as start conversations and post photos. It will take some time, but you will want to engage often so that the conversations can lead to real life encounters. This may mean meeting at an event, a party or at some social situations (never alone). You want to bring the online friendship and network into the real world.

I met a broker online who has been an invaluable resource. He has opened many doors for me that I never could have opened on my own, such as; introductions to private money lenders, title companies, networking events, tours, and so forth. I also received a listing from a Facebook friend who saw a post of me with my son that simply said, "In Center City Philadelphia." She reached out immediately and wrote, "I didn't know you were living and working in Philadelphia. I have two homes in Philadelphia that I want to sell."

2. *Be Omnipresent.* Attend local events such as street fairs, parties, sporting events, local concerts and even garage sales. Having a presence in the neighborhoods you represent lets people get to know you. Hand

out your cards, invitations to your Open House, fliers and become the person who they think of when they are selling their homes.

3. *Set up Super Open Houses.* A great Open House isn't as easy as having the signs and balloons all over the place. It takes a bit of orchestrating, with prep work and a positive attitude to get it right.

∞ ∞ ∞

The Super Open House

There are some decisions that can cost you greatly or even end your real estate career. In the beginning, I made a lot of new agent mistakes and learned a great deal from each one of them. One was working with buyers ineffectively (which I'll discuss later) and another was conducting a poor Open House.

The assistant managing broker at Weichert was a huge fan of Open House(s) to generate new business. Therefore, because she was my mentor, I began setting up Open Houses right away. Most were uneventful in the beginning. I failed to see the benefit of sitting around for two hours waiting for potential buyers. I preferred spending my time on the phone acquiring new listing appointments. However, I hung in there and eventually learned the secret to a successful Open House.

The first income I generated from an Open House was from a beautiful three level home in the Elkins Park area, in the suburbs of Philadelphia. I had acquired the listing a few weeks prior and I was sitting my second Open House. I met a young couple who loved the home. I immediately took down their contact information and followed up within 24 hours of the Open House. I scheduled an in-office meeting and, at that meeting, acquired all their documents to move forward. Unfortunately, they were unable to purchase, but within several months they reached out to me to list a home that they had just renovated. I ultimately sold that home for top dollar and I am now in the process of selling another one of their homes.

What made the difference? How did I go from sitting in an empty house for most of the two hours, to having successful open houses? For one thing, I would put up at least eight signs in busy traffic areas around the neighborhood to advertise the open house and put out several bunches of balloons around the front yard. In addition, I had teenagers pass out fliers the day of the Open House. I baked cookies, a pie, or cinnamon buns to spread a delicious smell throughout the home. Besides smelling delicious, the aroma of baked goods can trigger fond memories of childhood, or simply make people feel good. I would also prepare for the open house by cold calling the neighborhood and inviting them to attend. Then, once the guests arrived, I would welcome them, have them sign in (and provide their email addresses and phone numbers so I could follow-up with them, which is very important). Finally, I send them on their way to tour the house. I would also make an effort to talk to each attendee and answer their questions. But I would try not to spend too long with any one person, or couple, so I could interact with everyone.

Before leaving the open house, I would then give out gift bags with property information, company giveaways, toys, Christmas gifts, Easter baskets, etc. The key, I learned, is doing something to stand out from the rest. It is all about making the event memorable and giving the people a positive experience, so they will feel good about the house. It's important to be positive, engaging and encouraging.

Tips for an Awesome Open House Include:

1. *Print up beautifully designed fliers, highlighting the best features of the home, which can be very helpful.* I recommend that you use the services that the broker provides for fliers and advertisements because there are rules that must be followed when it comes to real estate advertising and your agency can help you learn such rules in your state or city. At Weichert, I can create an unlimited amount of free color fliers and print as many as I want for no charge.

2. *Hire a professional photographer—this is a must.* A pro can see hidden beauty and unique features that when presented on the internet will attract the attention of multiple buyers. Look at house photos online, see what other real estate agents are showing and ask around for the recommendation of a good photographer. BUT, you don't need to go overboard with the best in the business. Just find someone who takes good photos at a price you can afford. Do the same with a video. Find someone who knows how to take a good video.

3. *Post an ad on Craigslist.* This can be a simple ad with the key information—nothing elaborate. Make sure this runs in the local area for the week leading up to the Open House.

4. *Put your signs up early in the week.* Remember to include local bulletin boards and even stores if it's okay with the owner or manager. Keep the signs simple. Take them down after the event so you can use them again.

5. *Hold a broker tour or invite other agents from your office to a preview.* You do this to see if you're making the best impression on potential buyers. You don't want to overlook anything. Get some feedback from other pros.

6. *Get feedback,* so you'll know what you are doing well and what you need to improve. Before guests leave, I ask for feedback. In doing so, I get into a conversation and then slowly build a rapport to the point that I am setting up appointments for them to meet me in my office. This once led to making a sale directly from an Open House. They were ready to buy before the Open House was over. But that is very rare. Most Open House guests are just looking around and tire kicking, without an agent breathing down their neck.

I have picked up a lot of buyers and some sellers from open houses. Sellers like my presentation and have often hired me based on the professional job that I have done for their neighbors. This is why you invite people from the neighborhood to the Open House. Buyer's like my laid-back style and the fact that I'm full of information about the buying process. I even met a buyer during an Open House that was quite impressed with my gift bag. She told me that she had attended many open houses but had never been to one that had so many of the details covered. She was also impressed with my knowledge of real estate. I never found her a home to purchase, but she did reach out to me weeks later to sell one of the homes she owned. Now, less than a year later I'm in the process of selling another one of her homes.

Being the best in real estate sales means you must master the art of marketing, prospecting and constantly following up. You must stay in open communications with your clients, and never give up when things are going bad. It's advantageous to start out on the right foot and do things correctly from the beginning. For this reason, I decided to write this book in hopes of helping new agents skip some of the pitfalls.

All the work I do to plan an Open House, as mentioned above, needs to be coordinated in advance. After you acquire the listing you should immediately process the paperwork, schedule the professional photographer, upload the listing accurately to the MLS, put up your for-sale sign and lockbox, and schedule the Open House for the next Sunday. Do not wait to do this. If it is a holiday, or Super Bowl Sunday, I then aim for the following week, but I do not delay any longer than that. You also need to set up the specific time of day so that people aren't wandering in from sunrise to sunset, or later. Typically, you set up the Open House for two or three hours on a Sunday afternoon.

DEBORAH ANN SPENCE

Push forward and be extremely diligent early on. This will save you a lot of aggravation going forward, such as incorrect listings, bad photos, no entry plan to see the listing, and so on. You don't want to appear to be unprofessional which can potentially get you pulled from the listing. Also, lazy or sloppy work will assure that you do not receive a referral for future business and can potentially lead to bad reviews on the internet. You want to work hard and get the listing sold in a month if possible.

As for expenses, they are not usually very high. The signs are an expense that will typically come from your pocket. What I did, when I was first starting out, was use the signs left behind in the office by people who were no longer with the company. I'd put a label across the sign if necessary or use a generic sign with just the office phone number. You also need lockboxes, which are usually another expense for you, as is the photographer, unless you know someone personally who takes very high-quality photos. While you don't want to spend a lot, keep in mind that whatever you spend is all worthwhile when you make the sale. Don't skimp on these things. They can pay off in the end.

It's also important to establish a very good relationship with the home owners. If they see you as the professional you are, they will trust you and listen to your advice. If the home owner is in control, or tries to be in control, you will be in an ongoing battle, which will make it very difficult to sell the home. I can tell during the initial house tour when the seller is trying to control the situation. For example, if I ask the sellers to sit in the kitchen so we can discuss the house and they say we should to sit someplace else, I can see that they are going to try to be in control of this whole relationship. You will then find yourself going back and forth on everything, which slows down the process.

To establish control, I bring information from my manager about the company and plenty of information about the real estate market. I want to be able to support whatever I say with facts and figures. It shows that I am the professional—the expert—and that I know my job. I also speak with confidence, which I gain from doing my research and staying up to date on the industry, plus double checking my facts and figures. If the seller knows more about your business than you do, you will not be able to gain control of the situation. Too many new agents forget that the sellers also have access to the internet and may find all sorts of information. Do your research and dig a little deeper through the resources at your agency, and the books you have, even the books you used to study for your exams (remember them?). This way you are always one step ahead of the sellers. And, if you are asked a question and do not have an answer available, don't guess, fumble, or make something up. Tell them, "I'll check on that and get the answer shortly." Then find the answer!

By having resources and keeping abreast of the industry they can see that it's not just Deborah Spence giving them advice, but it's also coming from various other sources.

∞ ∞ ∞

DEBORAH ANN SPENCE

Keep the Sellers Busy

As for the sellers, before the Open House, you want to have them lock up their valuables, to play it safe, and straighten up the house so visitors are not tripping over their "stuff" as they walk around. They should also make sure the grounds are not a mess and the grass has been cut. Curb appeal counts.

Some sellers will then want to be around and/or involved on the day of the Open House. If they are around, keep them busy; find some tasks they can do. If they want to be "involved" with the buyers, it can become a problem. Sellers, while they think they are being helpful, can create an awkward situation.

I had a seller in the house when a young couple came in and had questions about the property. The homeowner told them that they looked really young and asked if they could afford the house, because it was very expensive. Obviously, being judged as *unable to afford the house because of their age* turned off the buyers. They finished the tour and, right before they left, the young man told the seller that his parents were going to pay for the house, but after his comment, they were no longer interested. Truth is; sellers can say some dumb stuff.

Therefore, you want to keep the sellers busy on the day of the Open House, so they won't be in the middle of the activity all day. One agent noted that she sent her sellers to the theater. A little bit costly, but *perhaps,* not a bad idea.

Burning Desire

∞ ∞ ∞

Safety at Open Houses

Not every open house is a success story and not every open house is without risk. I held an Open House in a very sketchy part of town and encountered a "guest," or intruder, who was high on some type of drug and was acting very erratically. He came into the Open House and began by licking the floor, which gave me reason for concern. Then he approached me, and I believe he wanted to rob me. But being a sometimes-sharp New York City girl, I quickly called someone to come over to help. FYI, the police do not show up in sketchy neighborhoods unless you're reporting gunshots. So, I made a quick call on my cell phone to a friend, but I told the floor-licker that I was calling security and that they patrolled the block every half hour. It took a moment or two, but my friend caught on that this was a troublesome situation. Meanwhile, believing that security was on the way, the guy got scared and left even before she showed up.

I called myself a "sometimes sharp New York City girl" because I was once robbed in Philadelphia. I lost a chunk of vacation cash I was carrying, a brand-new Microsoft Surface laptop, designer bag, wallet, credit cards, real estate tools and equipment, and more. Why? Because I wasn't paying attention, so my bag was snatched, and the culprit ran. As real estate agents, we are often targets. But that will not happen to be again. I am very much more alert now when I go into any neighborhood and hold an Open House, whether I am in the city or a suburb.

You need to be careful with what you are taking with you and have all your computer/phone data backed up someplace, such as the cloud. You can replace credit cards, your phone, a laptop and a bag, but your contact lists and data are very hard to replace, as is cash, so try not to carry too much at any time or take too much to an Open House.

The personal safety concern with an Open House is that you are inside of a location where people can (and are even invited to) walk in and look around. To be safe at an Open House, or at any other showing, I recommend the following:

- Stay by the door and let the guests walk around the house, telling them you are waiting for other attendees.

- Let someone in your office and a good friend or family member know where you will be and when.

- Carry a flashlight, small pocket knife, razor cutter, small stick, or small siren.

- Leave your personal items, except your phone, in the trunk of your car

- Keep your phone in your possession always and carry a small secondary phone in a discreet location. I like to keep a flip phone in my sock or in my Fannie Pack. Also make sure you have an emergency pre-programmed 911 number for the police

• Don't go into a room ahead of your guests so they can't follow you in and lock, or block the door, and never go to the basement or attic with a guest.

• Have people check large bags or anything they could use to steal items, at the front table near you, at the entrance.

• You might have a friend at the open house just as an extra set of eyes. You could also have another agent with you. If you work in pairs, split the leads.

• Always know how many people are in the house. Check off people as they leave. This means if ten people have signed in and eight have left, two people are somewhere in the house. Be aware and be careful. Rather than walking around and looking for them, you can always get their cell phone numbers as they enter and text them.

• Park your car as close as possible. If you need to park a little farther away from the house, find a well-lit location.

The last thing I want to say on the topic is: Please do not become discouraged and make safety an excuse for failing in this business. You can become very successful in real estate, just as I have done but you must take some precautions.

∞ ∞ ∞

A few other general tips on open houses

- Price the home slightly below market cost.

- Offer an incentive, like a free 50-inch television with first full price offer.

- Don't let too many people in the home at any one time. Let people know they may have to wait before entering. You need to have control over what's going on.

- Start blogging. I've learned recently that blogging about the open house, or simply about the listing (or both) can be helpful. Write 10 to 20 short (2-3 paragraph) blogs about your listing.

∞ ∞ ∞

Buyers

If you're going to be a real estate agent, you'll need to learn to work with the other half of the equation…the buyers.

Working with buyers is, in one significant way, the same as working with sellers; you need to know their motivation. You must figure out the core reason why they want to buy a home. Are they looking for more room, downsizing, looking for a neighborhood closer to work, closer to the schools, Closer to relatives, an apartment with a better view, or relocating because of a new job? The only way to find out is to ask them. Find out why they are looking for a new home.

Burning Desire

As a new agent, I was afraid of buyers. I had heard so many bad stories about them. Some agents and trainers had said that "buyers are liars," that they are not loyal, and that they can file complaints against you for no reason, which can cause you great distress. Not only was I afraid of buyers because of the stories that I heard and read, but I was afraid that, in person, it would be difficult because of my social awkwardness, or because my New York accent would come out. I was also scared that my inexperience would show.

Working with sellers, primarily over the phone, and with short meetings and brief ten-minute interactions to get paperwork signed, never worried me. However, I knew that working with buyers would mean a lot more personal interaction. You must meet them in the office and find out their motivation, explain the buying process, review homes on the market and then take them out several times to see home after home after home after home after home after.... well you get the point. Then, you must work with them to write up the agreement of sale, handle the home inspections, the walk-throughs, negotiations, the lender documents, the buyer's remorse, and on and on and on. The interaction with buyers can almost be endless until a settlement, aka closing, takes place, which can sometimes be as many as nine months after the initial consultation. Nonetheless, being the positive person that I am, I learned how to work with buyers.

Yes, working with buyers can be a positive experience. BUT, you need to set some parameters and remain in control, much as you have to do with sellers. At the first meeting I will find out as much as I can about the buyers using a list of questions.

My questions are:

- Where do you want to live?

- Where do you live now?

- Did you find any homes on the internet that you like?

- Do you have an agent?

- Have you signed any contracts with an agent?

- Are you a first-time home buyer?

- When do you want to buy?

- Are you currently renting?

- Are you pre-approved for a mortgage?

- Do you have any credit problems?

- Will anyone be giving you the down payment funds?

- How much do you want your mortgage to be per month?

- Are you the only one making the decisions?

- Are you afraid to start the process to buy?

- How quickly can you act, if I found you the perfect house?

- Have you had any good or bad experiences with real estate agents?

- What are the "must haves" in your new home?

- Are you willing to hire me as your real estate agent?

- How can I help you?

The above questions help get to the buyer's motivation and save you (the agent) a lot of time and aggravation by knowing if they are ready, willing and able to buy before you spend so much time with them.

Of course, I do ask about the buyer's price range. However, I prefer that they meet with a mortgage consultant to determine what they can afford. I also remind them to please try and remember that buying is a process of elimination, not a process of selection. You need to eliminate the houses that don't have what you want and those that are simply out of your price range. Buyers will often learn that they may not get everything they could possibly want in their price range. Therefore, they need to think about what is really most important to them What are their priorities? What is motivating them? Then they must let you know.

When I first started out, I would shuttle buyers around all the time. I recall taking buyers from one home to the next, spending hours, days, weeks, and months before getting the answers to many of the questions above. One couple was eager to purchase before January. During the holiday season, we saw at least 40 homes—sometimes as many as ten per day. By the end of the year, we narrowed it down to one home. We spent the entire day taking measurements and looking over every inch of the house. The couple left satisfied with their decision and asked me to draw up the full price offer. We were to meet again that evening to sign the documents. Before the documents were finalized, however, the couple called and asked if they could bring a friend as they want to see the house one last time. I agreed and returned to the house with the couple and their friend. The friend looked around the place and then proceeded to talk the couple out of buying the house. He didn't like it. If I would have known from the beginning that the friend was also a decision maker, I would have asked that he come along on all the showings.

After the initial shock and disappointment wore off, reality kicked in. "I said this business is hard, and buyers can be brutal." Then, I called a friend and whined and complained. But, as soon as I hung up, I hugged my son and went for a walk. That turned into a jog. That turned into a sprint. I returned home tired, hungry, and sweaty, but most important I came home with an attitude of, "I'm not giving up." I refuse to be defeated. I also asked myself why I was complaining and whining when it was my job to find out if another decision maker needed to be involved from the very beginning. That was my job and I failed. So, from that experience forward, each time I worked with a buyer I got better and better. Now, I'm pretty good at it.

How do I meet buyers?

As I mentioned earlier, the company I work for, Weichert, has a lead network system, which has buyers contact an 800 number and agents get back to them quickly. Other agencies have their own means of advertising and reaching out to buyers. You'll also attract buyers with your own website or page, not to mention blogs and comments on social media—answering questions and posting current articles of interest to buyers. Even a paragraph of content here and there can generate interest. It's also important that people see photos or videos on your site—homes you've sold, homes for sale, anything that captures the attention of prospective buyers. People go to the internet to find what they want. In fact, Realtor.com® noted that 75% of buyer inquiries are obtained online. So, make sure you have a presence, update it, and stay current.

And, while I shouldn't even have to mention this, get back to buyers quickly. Too many agents lose buyers by responding late, or not at all. Things move quickly today, that means if you want to be in the game, you must respond to emails, texts or phone calls quickly. I always make it a priority to get back to buyers, or sellers, as fast as possible. This goes beyond the first impression; it's just a good business practice. To maintain a good relationship, you cannot disappear. Neither buyers nor sellers want a real estate agent that is hard to get in touch with—and in an age of cell phones, that should not be the case.

As for buyer agent commissions, it can be 50% of the commission the seller agreed to pay. So, if it's a 6% commission, the buyer agent will receive 3%. But commission payout is not standard; it's all up to negotiating with the seller's agent. Your broker (remember, you are working under a broker) will collect the commission that you will receive, and you will be paid shortly after (3-4 days). There were times that I was paid 1.5% or 2%, but that was better than zero, and in my first year, I could not afford to turn anything down. I accepted everything that was given after the negotiation of course. Since then, I've improved my negotiation skills.

Working with a buyer can take a lot of time if you do not know the buyer's needs and expectations. First, you should make sure that they're qualified to purchase a house whether it's cash or mortgage. This means that they are pre-approved for a mortgage by a lender, which is typically based on their income, assets and any regular commitments against their income. If they are not pre-approved, I put them in touch with an in-house lender or another mortgage broker that I know (and with whom I am comfortable).

Once a buyer is qualified, I now do a consultation. In my first year, I would then drive them around to 50 or 100 houses. But, I don't do that anymore. Instead, during the consultation, I show them listings of about 40 or 50 houses and ask them to choose 20 of the best that meet most of their qualifications. Then I ask what would be the top ten...then we go to see the top five on that list to see if one meets all the criteria that they want. I also bring the documents in case they see the one they really want. I look for people who are serious about buying and aren't just going to keep looking and looking and looking....I try to streamline the process because you can waste so much time with buyers. You need to try to get people to narrow down their choices sooner than later. Real buyers have a good idea of what they want from the beginning.

No, most people won't buy the first house they see, or any house, on that first day, but I do want buyers who are ready to commit in the next ten days to a month.

Personally, I prefer spending my time cold calling sellers. My condition, although much better than in the past, still sometimes causes me to get a little lost when driving to multiple locations, even with the help of a GPS.

There are people who love working with buyers and those who prefer working with sellers. In fact, there are companies that give new hires personality tests to find out if they are a good fit to work as a listing agent, buyer agent, or as an inside sales agent. Keller Williams uses two behavioral assessments: the DISC and the AVA. The DISC looks at four major behavioral styles: Dominance, Influencer, Steadiness, and Compliance. While the format varies by provider, questions are often some version of, "Here is a list of four terms. Which is most like you and which is the least like you?" If so, why? The AVA identifies natural tendencies and workplace behaviors.

No matter which side you are working with, sellers or buyers, you will need to be encouraging (the process can be scary for buyers and sellers). You need to understand their motivation, have some empathy and some patience. This is not the profession for you, if you are very confrontational. No matter how marvelous a house may appear (even if it meets all the expectations, wants and needs on their checklist), the buyers may still find something they don't like. Arguing with them isn't going to make a difference.

Like anything worthwhile, working with buyers can be challenging. If you go into it with the sell, sell, sell and make a buck mindset, you may struggle. After all, you're not selling them a $50, $100 or even $500 appliance. You're helping them buy, or sell, what is most likely the biggest asset they have—not to mention something that will play a significant role in the life of the individual, couple or family moving out or, or moving into—their home.

Therefore, you need to focus on doing what is best for them, and if you can master the art of selling houses for fair prices, or more, and putting buyers into a home they will love, the money will follow as your reputation grows. And yes, it can be very exciting—even an adrenaline rush when you help them buy, or sell, a home.

Chapter 5

Moving Forward

SO, MY FRIENDS AND FUTURE REAL estate agents, it's no longer about "what to do." At this point, you should know the basics of what to do to get yourself started and to hopefully become successful in your first year. Of course, there is a lot more detailed information that you can find on the internet, in books and from seminars (or webinars). Remember, you need to embrace learning if you want to really succeed.

But it's not just *"what to do,"* that matters. It's about how you approach your new career. Remember, you need to know why you are embarking on this new journey, what your motivation is and what is your "why?" You need to have a passion for real estate and a burning desire no matter how many hours of prospecting for clients it takes to make it happen. You must also be organized (use a Google calendar for example) and have a relentless level of commitment. You must tell yourself that you are doing this no matter what.

If you follow the steps you will become a real estate agent. The question then is how far will you go? According to Realtor® Magazine, as of 2016, the median income for real estate agents was $42,500, which meant selling roughly a dozen homes. They also noted that approximately a quarter of real estate agents, mostly working part-time, make under $10,000 per year, while a quarter of the agents (the ones who are most dedicated I must assume) earn over $100,000 a year. The question is; do you have the burning desire to be in that top 25% or even the top 10%? I get the sense that if you're reading this book to seek knowledge on how to be successful in your first year in real estate sales, you are looking to move well-beyond being in the middle of the pack.

∞ ∞ ∞

Some reminders/tips to move forward more quickly:

First, establish a good rapport with sellers, buyers and pretty much everyone you meet. Listen to them, be empathetic, understanding, and provide them with the answers they need—be the experts.

Remember that buying or selling a house is a significant event for most people, so understand their anxiety and do not argue or lose your cool with clients.

Never ignore your phone or send callers to voicemail. I answer my cell phone 90% of the time unless I'm in a meeting or in an unsafe environment. But, even then, I answer and tell the contact that I will call them back and explain why. I am guilty of answering my phone in the early am, and sometimes even late at night when contacts who work late call me. Typically, they expect to reach a voicemail, and I surprise them with a bright "HELLO, this is Deborah!"

When they ask, "How are you?"

I say, "I'm Super Awesome! How can I help you?"

Do not take a vacation your first year. Yes, (if needed) take a day off, a long weekend, holidays, birthdays, events—of course. But do not take an extended vacation and become inaccessible. That is sudden death for your career. Why? You lose momentum and you lose focus. It takes weeks to get back into the rhythm of your duties. It's a bad decision, in my opinion, to take a vacation your first year. I did not. I stayed the course and just kept on pushing forward, looking at my motivation board as I toiled away. And, it paid off immensely.

Do not avoid prospecting. You must prospect even if it's uncomfortable, not your natural talent, unpleasant, boring, tiresome, annoying, and frustrating. You must continue every day. If you stop, you will fail.

Remember, the more "no(s)" you hear, the closer you are getting to a "yes," from someone who wants to list with you.

If you do not master the art of 'follow up,' you will fail. Buyers and sellers will very rarely make an immediate decision about what is one of the biggest decisions of their life: buying or selling a home. It takes time and a lot of mulling it over before they will give you a decision as to whether they want to move forward with a sale or a purchase. This is where the "follow up" part is key. You must call them, ask for permission to follow up, and then, continue doing so until they say "Yes," "Put me on the do not call list (DNC)," or answer with something explicit or hateful like "Drop dead," "You have the worst job ever," "You're pitiful," and such.

Finally, if you want to be an average agent, do the minimum and stop continuing your education and knowledge. Stop continuing to grow. But, if you want to grow your business and succeed, continue your quest for knowledge about real estate, marketing, law, mortgages, technology, business, accounting, taxes, budgeting, appraisals, investments, development, commercial real estate, management, lenders, finances, teams, certifications, specialties, and other interesting topics.

Don't fear technology. I have seen agents struggle with technology. It doesn't matter if they are old, young, or middle age. Some agents have a hard time navigating the use of the technology tools that we use, and I find it amazing how they lack the desire to take classes to learn how to master these tools. If I am a carpenter and I don't know how to use a hammer, then I am a very ineffective carpenter. Take the time to learn the tools, practice using them and before you know it you will be proficient in the tools of the trade.

It Gets Easier!

Lastly, I have good news for all of you aspiring real estate agents who are studying for your real estate licensing exams as well as newly licensed agents and those of you working in your rookie year. Even if you have been struggling for a few years to get up and running, let me tell you—IT GETS EASIER! Yes, the hardship will not last forever. I have personally witnessed agents who have started out very slowly but managed to hang in there and prosper. They have grown, slowly at first and then more quickly. I have seen them in my office, talked to agents from other companies, and have received emails (or calls) from agents across the country who have updated me on their success stories.

If you work hard, put in the hours and stay committed to your business it will get easier. Too many folks give up too quickly. This is true in so many business ventures. People don't stay the course. They quit because they don't see immediate results. But, by hanging in there, always referring to why you are doing this, and keeping in mind that this is a career over which you have a lot of control, you will see things getting easier. By my second year, I was getting referrals from people I met in my first year. Therefore, I was making fewer cold calls and getting more business. As I sold more homes, and more people wanted to work with me, I built a reputation for being good at what I do. I was then able to do less marketing and more selling. That's how I went from 63 listings and 31 sales in my first year up to 49 sales in my second year. Success builds on success. This is how you build a referral business.

In my second year, I can honestly say my phone rang more times and I found myself prospecting much less. All the energy, passion, dedication, and commitment that I put forth in the first year of my career spilled over into my second. And now, in my third year, I continue to see this incredible snowball effect that can be overwhelming at times.

I have been able to do things that I would have never imagined possible. Sometimes thinking about such things brings a little tear to my eyes, like right now. This real estate business is a massive opportunity to break down barriers, change lives, open an immense world of knowledge, fulfill dreams, end poverty, motivate, and inspire. I hope that I have "fired you up" to get you moving forward to sell real estate. Most importantly, I hope that I have shared with you the reality that anyone can be successful in the real estate sales business.

Remember, if I managed to become successful, you can too. Good luck and please share with me your hopes, dreams and success stories. Also, ask me questions if you want.

My website is http://www.deborahspencesoldit.com.

My personal email address is deborahspnc@yahoo.com.

Books & Documents

Recommended for Motivation, Inspiration, and Knowledge

The Code of Ethics by National Association of REALTORS®

Dream Big by Cristiane Correa

Expired Listings by David Rodwell

Fanatical Prospecting by Jeb Blount

First a Dream by Jim Clayton

Iacocca: An Autobiography by Lee Iacocca and William Novak

The Miracle Morning for Real Estate Agents: It's your time to rise and shine by   Hal Elrod, Michael J Maher, Michael Reese, & Jay Kinder

No Excuses by Brian Tracy

Real: A Path to Passion, Purpose and Profits in Real Estate by Dave Crumby, Martin Streiche, & Lani Rosales

Relentless: From Good to Great by Tim S. Grover

The Real Estate Agents Guide to FSBOs by John Maloof

The Standard Agreement of Sale by Pennsylvania Association of Realtors®

Think and Grow Rich by Napoleon Hill

Time Management by Brian Tracy

Tools of Titans by Tim Ferriss

Appendix

Code of Ethics and Standards of Practice
of the National Association of REALTORS®

Effective January 1, 2018

Where the word REALTORS® is used in this Code and Preamble, it shall be deemed to include REALTOR-ASSOCIATE®s.

While the Code of Ethics establishes obligations that may be higher than those mandated by law, in any instance where the Code of Ethics and the law conflict, the obligations of the law must take precedence.

Preamble

Under all is the land. Upon its wise utilization and widely allocated ownership depend the survival and growth of free institutions and of our civilization. REALTORS® should recognize that the interests of the nation and its citizens require the highest and best use of the land and the widest distribution of land ownership. They require the creation of adequate housing, the building of functioning cities, the development of productive industries and farms, and the preservation of a healthful environment.

Such interests impose obligations beyond those of ordinary commerce. They impose grave social responsibility and a patriotic duty to which REALTORS® should dedicate themselves, and for which they should be diligent in preparing themselves. REALTORS®, therefore, are zealous to maintain and improve the standards of their calling and share with their fellow REALTORS® a common responsibility for its integrity and honor.

In recognition and appreciation of their obligations to clients, customers, the public, and each other, REALTORS® continuously strive to become and remain informed on issues affecting real estate and, as knowledgeable professionals, they willingly share the fruit of their experience and study with others. They identify and take steps, through enforcement of this Code of Ethics and by assisting appropriate regulatory bodies, to eliminate practices which may damage the public or which might discredit or bring dishonor to the real estate profession. REALTORS® having direct personal knowledge of conduct that may violate the Code of Ethics involving misappropriation of client or customer funds or property, willful discrimination, or fraud resulting in substantial economic harm, bring such matters to the attention of the appropriate Board or Association of REALTORS®. *(Amended 1/00)*

Realizing that cooperation with other real estate professionals promotes the best interests of those who utilize their services, REALTORS® urge exclusive representation of clients; do not attempt to gain any unfair advantage over their competitors; and they refrain from making unsolicited comments about other practitioners. In instances where their opinion is sought, or where REALTORS® believe that comment is necessary, their opinion is offered in an objective, professional manner, uninfluenced by any personal motivation or potential advantage or gain.

The term REALTOR® has come to connote competency, fairness, and high integrity resulting from adherence to a lofty ideal of moral conduct in business relations. No inducement of profit and no instruction from clients ever can justify departure from this ideal.

In the interpretation of this obligation, REALTORS® can take no safer guide than that which has been handed down through the centuries, embodied in the Golden Rule, "Whatsoever ye would that others should do to you, do ye even so to them."

Accepting this standard as their own, REALTORS® pledge to observe its spirit in all of their activities whether conducted personally, through associates or others, or via technological means, and to conduct their business in accordance with the tenets set forth below. *(Amended 1/07)* [listen]

Duties to Clients and Customers

Article 1 (Case Interpretations for Article 1)

When representing a buyer, seller, landlord, tenant, or other client as an agent, REALTORS® pledge themselves to protect and promote the interests of their client. This obligation to the client is primary, but it does not relieve REALTORS® of their obligation to treat all parties honestly. When serving a buyer, seller, landlord, tenant or other party in a non-agency capacity, REALTORS® remain obligated to treat all parties honestly. *(Amended 1/01)* [listen]

- Standard of Practice 1-1

  REALTORS®, when acting as principals in a real estate transaction, remain obligated by the duties imposed by the Code of Ethics. *(Amended 1/93)*

- Standard of Practice 1-2

  The duties imposed by the Code of Ethics encompass all real estate-related activities and transactions whether conducted in person, electronically, or through any other means.

  The duties the Code of Ethics imposes are applicable whether REALTORS® are acting as agents or in legally recognized non-agency capacities except that any duty imposed exclusively on agents by law or regulation shall not be imposed by this Code of Ethics on REALTORS® acting in non-agency capacities.

  As used in this Code of Ethics, "client" means the person(s) or entity(ies) with whom a REALTOR® or a REALTOR®'s firm has an agency or legally recognized non-agency relationship; "customer" means a party to a real estate transaction who receives information, services, or benefits but has no contractual relationship with the REALTOR® or the REALTOR®'s firm; "prospect" means a purchaser, seller, tenant, or landlord who is not subject to a representation relationship with the REALTOR® or REALTOR®'s firm; "agent" means a real estate licensee (including brokers and sales associates) acting in an agency relationship as defined by state law or regulation; and "broker" means a real estate licensee (including brokers and sales associates) acting as an agent or in a legally recognized non-agency capacity. *(Adopted 1/95, Amended 1/07)*

- Standard of Practice 1-3

     REALTORS®, in attempting to secure a listing, shall not deliberately mislead the owner as to market value.

- Standard of Practice 1-4

     REALTORS®, when seeking to become a buyer/tenant representative, shall not mislead buyers or tenants as to savings or other benefits that might be realized through use of the REALTOR®'s services. *(Amended 1/93)*

- Standard of Practice 1-5

     REALTORS® may represent the seller/landlord and buyer/tenant in the same transaction only after full disclosure to and with informed consent of both parties. *(Adopted 1/93)*

- Standard of Practice 1-6

     REALTORS® shall submit offers and counter-offers objectively and as quickly as possible. *(Adopted 1/93, Amended 1/95)*

- Standard of Practice 1-7

     When acting as listing brokers, REALTORS® shall continue to submit to the seller/landlord all offers and counter-offers until closing or execution of a lease unless the seller/landlord has waived this obligation in writing. REALTORS® shall not be obligated to continue to market the property after an offer has been accepted by the seller/landlord. REALTORS® shall recommend that sellers/landlords obtain the advice of legal counsel prior to acceptance of a subsequent offer except where the acceptance is contingent on the termination of the pre-existing purchase contract or lease. *(Amended 1/93)*

- Standard of Practice 1-8

  REALTORS® , acting as agents or brokers of buyers/tenants, shall submit to buyers/tenants all offers and counter-offers until acceptance but have no obligation to continue to show properties to their clients after an offer has been accepted unless otherwise agreed in writing. REALTORS®, acting as agents or brokers of buyers/tenants, shall recommend that buyers/tenants obtain the advice of legal counsel if there is a question as to whether a pre-existing contract has been terminated. *(Adopted 1/93, Amended 1/99)*

- Standard of Practice 1-9

  The obligation of REALTORS® to preserve confidential information (as defined by state law) provided by their clients in the course of any agency relationship or non-agency relationship recognized by law continues after termination of agency relationships or any non-agency relationships recognized by law. REALTORS® shall not knowingly, during or following the termination of professional relationships with their clients:

1. reveal confidential information of clients; or

2. use confidential information of clients to the disadvantage of clients; or

3. use confidential information of clients for the REALTOR®'s advantage or the advantage of third parties unless:

   o a) clients consent after full disclosure; or

   o b) REALTORS® are required by court order; or

- c) it is the intention of a client to commit a crime and the information is necessary to prevent the crime; or

- d) it is necessary to defend a REALTOR® or the REALTOR®'s employees or associates against an accusation of wrongful conduct.

Information concerning latent material defects is not considered confidential information under this Code of Ethics. *(Adopted 1/93, Amended 1/01)*

- Standard of Practice 1-10

  REALTORS® shall, consistent with the terms and conditions of their real estate licensure and their property management agreement, competently manage the property of clients with due regard for the rights, safety and health of tenants and others lawfully on the premises. *(Adopted 1/95, Amended 1/00)*

- Standard of Practice 1-11

  REALTORS® who are employed to maintain or manage a client's property shall exercise due diligence and make reasonable efforts to protect it against reasonably foreseeable contingencies and losses. *(Adopted 1/95)*

- Standard of Practice 1-12

  When entering into listing contracts, REALTORS® must advise sellers/landlords of:

  1. the REALTOR®'s company policies regarding cooperation and the amount(s) of any compensation that will be offered to subagents, buyer/tenant agents, and/or brokers acting in legally recognized non-agency capacities;

2. the fact that buyer/tenant agents or brokers, even if compensated by listing brokers, or by sellers/landlords may represent the interests of buyers/tenants; and

3. any potential for listing brokers to act as disclosed dual agents, e.g. buyer/tenant agents. *(Adopted 1/93, Renumbered 1/98, Amended 1/03)*

- Standard of Practice 1-13

  When entering into buyer/tenant agreements, REALTORS® must advise potential clients of:

  1. the REALTOR®'s company policies regarding cooperation;

  2. the amount of compensation to be paid by the client;

  3. the potential for additional or offsetting compensation from other brokers, from the seller or landlord, or from other parties;

  4. any potential for the buyer/tenant representative to act as a disclosed dual agent, e.g. listing broker, subagent, landlord's agent, etc., and

  5. the possibility that sellers or sellers' representatives may not treat the existence, terms, or conditions of offers as confidential unless confidentiality is required by law, regulation, or by any confidentiality agreement between the parties. *(Adopted 1/93, Renumbered 1/98, Amended 1/06)*

- Standard of Practice 1-14

  Fees for preparing appraisals or other valuations shall not be contingent upon the amount of the appraisal or valuation. *(Adopted 1/02)*

- Standard of Practice 1-15

    REALTORS®, in response to inquiries from buyers or cooperating brokers shall, with the sellers' approval, disclose the existence of offers on the property. Where disclosure is authorized, REALTORS® shall also disclose, if asked, whether offers were obtained by the listing licensee, another licensee in the listing firm, or by a cooperating broker. *(Adopted 1/03, Amended 1/09)*

- Standard of Practice 1-16

    REALTORS® shall not use, or permit or enable others to use, listed or managed property on terms or conditions other than those authorized by the owner or seller. *(Adopted 1/12)*

Article 2 (Case Interpretations for Article 2)

REALTORS® shall avoid exaggeration, misrepresentation, or concealment of pertinent facts relating to the property or the transaction. REALTORS® shall not, however, be obligated to discover latent defects in the property, to advise on matters outside the scope of their real estate license, or to disclose facts which are confidential under the scope of agency or non-agency relationships as defined by state law. *(Amended 1/00)* [listen]

- Standard of Practice 2-1

    REALTORS® shall only be obligated to discover and disclose adverse factors reasonably apparent to someone with expertise in those areas required by their real estate licensing authority. Article 2 does not impose upon the REALTOR® the obligation of expertise in other professional or technical disciplines. *(Amended 1/96)*

- Standard of Practice 2-2

    (Renumbered as Standard of Practice 1-12 1/98)

- Standard of Practice 2-3

    (Renumbered as Standard of Practice 1-13 1/98)

- Standard of Practice 2-4

    REALTORS® shall not be parties to the naming of a false consideration in any document, unless it be the naming of an obviously nominal consideration.

- Standard of Practice 2-5

    Factors defined as "non-material" by law or regulation or which are expressly referenced in law or regulation as not being subject to disclosure are considered not "pertinent" for purposes of Article 2. *(Adopted 1/93)*

Article 3 (Case Interpretations for Article 3)

REALTORS® shall cooperate with other brokers except when cooperation is not in the client's best interest. The obligation to cooperate does not include the obligation to share commissions, fees, or to otherwise compensate another broker. *(Amended 1/95)* [listen]

- Standard of Practice 3-1

    REALTORS®, acting as exclusive agents or brokers of sellers/ landlords, establish the terms and conditions of offers to cooperate. Unless expressly indicated in offers to cooperate, cooperating brokers may not assume that the offer of cooperation includes an offer of compensation. Terms of compensation, if any, shall be ascertained by cooperating brokers before beginning efforts to accept the offer of cooperation. *(Amended 1/99)*

- Standard of Practice 3-2

     Any change in compensation offered for cooperative services must be communicated to the other REALTOR® prior to the time that REALTOR® submits an offer to purchase/lease the property. After a REALTOR® has submitted an offer to purchase or lease property, the listing broker may not attempt to unilaterally modify the offered compensation with respect to that cooperative transaction. *(Amended 1/14)*

- Standard of Practice 3-3

     Standard of Practice 3-2 does not preclude the listing broker and cooperating broker from entering into an agreement to change cooperative compensation. *(Adopted 1/94)*

- Standard of Practice 3-4

     REALTORS®, acting as listing brokers, have an affirmative obligation to disclose the existence of dual or variable rate commission arrangements (i.e., listings where one amount of commission is payable if the listing broker's firm is the procuring cause of sale/lease and a different amount of commission is payable if the sale/lease results through the efforts of the seller/ landlord or a cooperating broker). The listing broker shall, as soon as practical, disclose the existence of such arrangements to potential cooperating brokers and shall, in response to inquiries from cooperating brokers, disclose the differential that would result in a cooperative transaction or in a sale/lease that results through the efforts of the seller/landlord. If the cooperating broker is a buyer/tenant representative, the buyer/tenant representative must disclose such information to their client before the client makes an offer to purchase or lease. *(Amended 1/02)*

- Standard of Practice 3-5

    It is the obligation of subagents to promptly disclose all pertinent facts to the principal's agent prior to as well as after a purchase or lease agreement is executed. *(Amended 1/93)*

- Standard of Practice 3-6

    REALTORS® shall disclose the existence of accepted offers, including offers with unresolved contingencies, to any broker seeking cooperation. *(Adopted 5/86, Amended 1/04)*

- Standard of Practice 3-7

    When seeking information from another REALTOR® concerning property under a management or listing agreement, REALTORS® shall disclose their REALTOR® status and whether their interest is personal or on behalf of a client and, if on behalf of a client, their relationship with the client. *(Amended 1/11)*

- Standard of Practice 3-8

    REALTORS® shall not misrepresent the availability of access to show or inspect a listed property. *(Amended 11/87)*

- Standard of Practice 3-9

    REALTORS® shall not provide access to listed property on terms other than those established by the owner or the listing broker. *(Adopted 1/10)*

- Standard of Practice 3-10

   The duty to cooperate established in Article 3 relates to the obligation to share information on listed property, and to make property available to other brokers for showing to prospective purchasers/tenants when it is in the best interests of sellers/landlords. *(Adopted 1/11)*

Article 4 (Case Interpretations for Article 4)

REALTORS® shall not acquire an interest in or buy or present offers from themselves, any member of their immediate families, their firms or any member thereof, or any entities in which they have any ownership interest, any real property without making their true position known to the owner or the owner's agent or broker. In selling property they own, or in which they have any interest, REALTORS® shall reveal their ownership or interest in writing to the purchaser or the purchaser's representative. *(Amended 1/00)* [listen]

- Standard of Practice 4-1

   For the protection of all parties, the disclosures required by Article 4 shall be in writing and provided by REALTORS® prior to the signing of any contract. *(Adopted 2/86)*

Article 5 (Case Interpretations for Article 5)

REALTORS® shall not undertake to provide professional services concerning a property or its value where they have a present or contemplated interest unless such interest is specifically disclosed to all affected parties. [listen]

Article 6 (Case Interpretations for Article 6)

REALTORS® shall not accept any commission, rebate, or profit on expenditures made for their client, without the client's knowledge and consent.

When recommending real estate products or services (e.g., homeowner's insurance, warranty programs, mortgage financing, title insurance, etc.), REALTORS® shall disclose to the client or customer to whom the recommendation is made any financial benefits or fees, other than real estate referral fees, the REALTOR® or REALTOR®'s firm may receive as a direct result of such recommendation. *(Amended 1/99)* [listen]

- Standard of Practice 6-1

     REALTORS® shall not recommend or suggest to a client or a customer the use of services of another organization or business entity in which they have a direct interest without disclosing such interest at the time of the recommendation or suggestion. *(Amended 5/88)*

Article 7 (Case Interpretations for Article 7)

In a transaction, REALTORS® shall not accept compensation from more than one party, even if permitted by law, without disclosure to all parties and the informed consent of the REALTOR®'s client or clients. *(Amended 1/93)* [listen]

Article 8 (Case Interpretations for Article 8)

REALTORS® shall keep in a special account in an appropriate financial institution, separated from their own funds, monies coming into their possession in trust for other persons, such as escrows, trust funds, clients' monies, and other like items. [listen]

Article 9 (Case Interpretations for Article 9)

REALTORS®, for the protection of all parties, shall assure whenever possible that all agreements related to real estate transactions including, but not limited to, listing and representation agreements, purchase contracts, and leases are in writing in clear and understandable language expressing the specific terms, conditions, obligations and commitments of the parties. A copy of each agreement shall be furnished to each party to such agreements upon their signing or initialing. *(Amended 1/04)* [listen]

- Standard of Practice 9-1

  For the protection of all parties, REALTORS® shall use reasonable care to ensure that documents pertaining to the purchase, sale, or lease of real estate are kept current through the use of written extensions or amendments. *(Amended 1/93)*

- Standard of Practice 9-2

  When assisting or enabling a client or customer in establishing a contractual relationship (e.g., listing and representation agreements, purchase agreements, leases, etc.) electronically, REALTORS® shall make reasonable efforts to explain the nature and disclose the specific terms of the contractual relationship being established prior to it being agreed to by a contracting party. *(Adopted 1/07)*

Duties to the Public

Article 10 (Case Interpretations for Article 10)

REALTORS® shall not deny equal professional services to any person for reasons of race, color, religion, sex, handicap, familial status, national origin, sexual orientation, or gender identity. REALTORS® shall not be parties to any plan or agreement to discriminate against a person or persons on the basis of race, color, religion, sex, handicap, familial status, national origin, sexual orientation, or gender identity. *(Amended 1/14)*

REALTORS®, in their real estate employment practices, shall not discriminate against any person or persons on the basis of race, color, religion, sex, handicap, familial status, national origin, sexual orientation, or gender identity. *(Amended 1/14)* [listen]

- Standard of Practice 10-1

  When involved in the sale or lease of a residence, REALTORS® shall not volunteer information regarding the racial, religious or ethnic composition of any neighborhood nor shall they engage in any activity which may result in panic selling, however, REALTORS® may provide other demographic information. *(Adopted 1/94, Amended 1/06)*

- Standard of Practice 10-2

  When not involved in the sale or lease of a residence, REALTORS® may provide demographic information related to a property, transaction or professional assignment to a party if such demographic information is (a) deemed by the REALTOR® to be needed to assist with or complete, in a manner consistent with Article 10, a real estate transaction or professional assignment and (b) is obtained or derived from a recognized, reliable, independent, and impartial source. The source of such information and any additions, deletions, modifications, interpretations, or other changes shall be disclosed in reasonable detail. *(Adopted 1/05, Renumbered 1/06)*

- Standard of Practice 10-3

  REALTORS® shall not print, display or circulate any statement or advertisement with respect to selling or renting of a property that indicates any preference, limitations or discrimination based on race, color, religion, sex, handicap, familial status, national origin, sexual orientation, or gender identity.*(Adopted 1/94, Renumbered 1/05 and 1/06, Amended 1/14)*

- Standard of Practice 10-4

  As used in Article 10 "real estate employment practices" relates to employees and independent contractors providing real estate-related services and the administrative and clerical staff directly supporting those individuals. *(Adopted 1/00, Renumbered 1/05 and 1/06)*

Article 11 (Case Interpretations for Article 11)

The services which REALTORS® provide to their clients and customers shall conform to the standards of practice and competence which are reasonably expected in the specific real estate disciplines in which they engage; specifically, residential real estate brokerage, real property management, commercial and industrial real estate brokerage, land brokerage, real estate appraisal, real estate counseling, real estate syndication, real estate auction, and international real estate.

REALTORS® shall not undertake to provide specialized professional services concerning a type of property or service that is outside their field of competence unless they engage the assistance of one who is competent on such types of property or service, or unless the facts are fully disclosed to the client. Any persons engaged to provide such assistance shall be so identified to the client and their contribution to the assignment should be set forth. *(Amended 1/10)* [listen]

- Standard of Practice 11-1

When REALTORS® prepare opinions of real property value or price they must:

1. be knowledgeable about the type of property being valued,

2. have access to the information and resources necessary to formulate an accurate opinion, and

3. be familiar with the area where the subject property is located

unless lack of any of these is disclosed to the party requesting the opinion in advance.

When an opinion of value or price is prepared other than in pursuit of a listing or to assist a potential purchaser in formulating a purchase offer, the opinion shall include the following unless the party requesting the opinion requires a specific type of report or different data set:

1. identification of the subject property

2. date prepared

3. defined value or price

4. limiting conditions, including statements of purpose(s) and intended user(s)

5. any present or contemplated interest, including the possibility of representing the seller/landlord or buyers/tenants

6. basis for the opinion, including applicable market data

7. if the opinion is not an appraisal, a statement to that effect

8. disclosure of whether and when a physical inspection of the property's exterior was conducted

9. disclosure of whether and when a physical inspection of the property's interior was conducted

10. disclosure of whether the REALTOR® has any conflicts of interest *(Amended 1/14)*

- Standard of Practice 11-2

    The obligations of the Code of Ethics in respect of real estate disciplines other than appraisal shall be interpreted and applied in accordance with the standards of competence and practice which clients and the public reasonably require to protect their rights and interests considering the complexity of the transaction, the availability of expert assistance, and, where the REALTOR® is an agent or subagent, the obligations of a fiduciary. *(Adopted 1/95)*

- Standard of Practice 11-3

    When REALTORS® provide consultive services to clients which involve advice or counsel for a fee (not a commission), such advice shall be rendered in an objective manner and the fee shall not be contingent on the substance of the advice or counsel given. If brokerage or transaction services are to be provided in addition to consultive services, a separate compensation may be paid with prior agreement between the client and REALTOR®. *(Adopted 1/96)*

- Standard of Practice 11-4

    The competency required by Article 11 relates to services contracted for between REALTORS® and their clients or customers; the duties expressly imposed by the Code of Ethics; and the duties imposed by law or regulation. *(Adopted 1/02)*

Article 12 (Case Interpretations for Article 12)

REALTORS® shall be honest and truthful in their real estate communications and shall present a true picture in their advertising, marketing, and other representations. REALTORS® shall ensure that their status as real estate professionals is readily apparent in their advertising, marketing, and other representations, and that the recipients of all real estate communications are, or have been, notified that those communications are from a real estate professional. *(Amended 1/08)* [listen]

- Standard of Practice 12-1

   REALTORS® may use the term "free" and similar terms in their advertising and in other representations provided that all terms governing availability of the offered product or service are clearly disclosed at the same time. *(Amended 1/97)*

- Standard of Practice 12-2

   REALTORS® may represent their services as "free" or without cost even if they expect to receive compensation from a source other than their client provided that the potential for the REALTOR® to obtain a benefit from a third party is clearly disclosed at the same time. *(Amended 1/97)*

- Standard of Practice 12-3

   The offering of premiums, prizes, merchandise discounts or other inducements to list, sell, purchase, or lease is not, in itself, unethical even if receipt of the benefit is contingent on listing, selling, purchasing, or leasing through the REALTOR® making the offer. However, REALTORS® must exercise care and candor in any such advertising or other public or private representations so that any party interested in receiving or otherwise benefiting from the REALTOR®'s offer will have clear, thorough, advance understanding of all the terms and conditions of the offer. The offering of any inducements to do business is subject to the limitations and restrictions of state law and the ethical obligations established by any applicable Standard of Practice. *(Amended 1/95)*

- Standard of Practice 12-4

  REALTORS® shall not offer for sale/lease or advertise property without authority. When acting as listing brokers or as subagents, REALTORS® shall not quote a price different from that agreed upon with the seller/landlord. *(Amended 1/93)*

- Standard of Practice 12-5

  Realtors® shall not advertise nor permit any person employed by or affiliated with them to advertise real estate services or listed property in any medium (e.g., electronically, print, radio, television, etc.) without disclosing the name of that Realtor®'s firm in a reasonable and readily apparent manner either in the advertisement or in electronic advertising via a link to a display with all required disclosures. *(Adopted 11/86, Amended 1/16)*

- Standard of Practice 12-6

  REALTORS®, when advertising unlisted real property for sale/lease in which they have an ownership interest, shall disclose their status as both owners/landlords and as REALTORS® or real estate licensees. *(Amended 1/93)*

- Standard of Practice 12-7

  Only REALTORS® who participated in the transaction as the listing broker or cooperating broker (selling broker) may claim to have "sold" the property. Prior to closing, a cooperating broker may post a "sold" sign only with the consent of the listing broker. *(Amended 1/96)*

- Standard of Practice 12-8

  The obligation to present a true picture in representations to the public includes information presented, provided, or displayed on REALTORS®' websites. REALTORS® shall use reasonable efforts to ensure that information on their websites is current. When it becomes apparent that information on a REALTOR®'s website is no longer current or accurate, REALTORS® shall promptly take corrective action. *(Adopted 1/07)*

- Standard of Practice 12-9

  REALTOR® firm websites shall disclose the firm's name and state(s) of licensure in a reasonable and readily apparent manner.

  Websites of REALTORS® and non-member licensees affiliated with a REALTOR® firm shall disclose the firm's name and that REALTOR®'s or non-member licensee's state(s) of licensure in a reasonable and readily apparent manner. *(Adopted 1/07)*

- Standard of Practice 12-10

  REALTORS®' obligation to present a true picture in their advertising and representations to the public includes Internet content, images, and the URLs and domain names they use, and prohibits REALTORS® from:

  1. engaging in deceptive or unauthorized framing of real estate brokerage websites;

2. manipulating (e.g., presenting content developed by others) listing and other content in any way that produces a deceptive or misleading result;

3. deceptively using metatags, keywords or other devices/methods to direct, drive, or divert Internet traffic; or

4. presenting content developed by others without either attribution or without permission, or

5. otherwise misleading consumers, including use of misleading images. *(Adopted 1/07, Amended 1/18)*

- Standard of Practice 12-11

    REALTORS® intending to share or sell consumer information gathered via the Internet shall disclose that possibility in a reasonable and readily apparent manner. *(Adopted 1/07)*

- Standard of Practice 12-12

    REALTORS® shall not:

    1. use URLs or domain names that present less than a true picture, or

    2. register URLs or domain names which, if used, would present less than a true picture. *(Adopted 1/08)*

- Standard of Practice 12-13

    The obligation to present a true picture in advertising, marketing, and representations allows REALTORS® to use and display only professional designations, certifications, and other credentials to which they are legitimately entitled. *(Adopted 1/08)*

Article 13 (Case Interpretations for Article 13)

REALTORS® shall not engage in activities that constitute the unauthorized practice of law and shall recommend that legal counsel be obtained when the interest of any party to the transaction requires it. [listen]

Article 14 (Case Interpretations for Article 14)

If charged with unethical practice or asked to present evidence or to cooperate in any other way, in any professional standards proceeding or investigation, REALTORS® shall place all pertinent facts before the proper tribunals of the Member Board or affiliated institute, society, or council in which membership is held and shall take no action to disrupt or obstruct such processes. *(Amended 1/99)* [listen]

- Standard of Practice 14-1

   REALTORS® shall not be subject to disciplinary proceedings in more than one Board of REALTORS® or affiliated institute, society or council in which they hold membership with respect to alleged violations of the Code of Ethics relating to the same transaction or event. *(Amended 1/95)*

- Standard of Practice 14-2

   REALTORS® shall not make any unauthorized disclosure or dissemination of the allegations, findings, or decision developed in connection with an ethics hearing or appeal or in connection with an arbitration hearing or procedural review. *(Amended 1/92)*

- Standard of Practice 14-3

REALTORS® shall not obstruct the Board's investigative or professional standards proceedings by instituting or threatening to institute actions for libel, slander or defamation against any party to a professional standards proceeding or their witnesses based on the filing of an arbitration request, an ethics complaint, or testimony given before any tribunal. *(Adopted 11/87, Amended 1/99)*

- Standard of Practice 14-4

    REALTORS® shall not intentionally impede the Board's investigative or disciplinary proceedings by filing multiple ethics complaints based on the same event or transaction. *(Adopted 11/88)*

Duties to REALTORS®

Article 15 (Case Interpretations for Article 15)

REALTORS® shall not knowingly or recklessly make false or misleading statements about other real estate professionals, their businesses, or their business practices. *(Amended 1/12)* [listen]

- Standard of Practice 15-1

    REALTORS® shall not knowingly or recklessly file false or unfounded ethics complaints. *(Adopted 1/00)*

- Standard of Practice 15-2

    The obligation to refrain from making false or misleading statements about other real estate professionals, their businesses and their business practices includes the duty to not knowingly or recklessly publish, repeat, retransmit, or republish false or misleading statements made by others. This duty applies whether false or misleading statements are repeated in person, in writing, by technological means (e.g., the Internet), or by any other means. *(Adopted 1/07, Amended 1/12)*

- Standard of Practice 15-3

  The obligation to refrain from making false or misleading statements about other real estate professionals, their businesses, and their business practices includes the duty to publish a clarification about or to remove statements made by others on electronic media the REALTOR® controls once the REALTOR® knows the statement is false or misleading. *(Adopted 1/10, Amended 1/12)*

Article 16 (Case Interpretations for Article 16)

REALTORS® shall not engage in any practice or take any action inconsistent with exclusive representation or exclusive brokerage relationship agreements that other REALTORS® have with clients. *(Amended 1/04)* [listen]

- Standard of Practice 16-1

  Article 16 is not intended to prohibit aggressive or innovative business practices which are otherwise ethical and does not prohibit disagreements with other REALTORS® involving commission, fees, compensation or other forms of payment or expenses. *(Adopted 1/93, Amended 1/95)*

- Standard of Practice 16-2

  Article 16 does not preclude REALTORS® from making general announcements to prospects describing their services and the terms of their availability even though some recipients may have entered into agency agreements or other exclusive relationships with another REALTOR®. A general telephone canvass, general mailing or distribution addressed to all prospects in a given geographical area or in a given profession, business, club, or organization, or other classification or group is deemed "general" for purposes of this standard. *(Amended 1/04)*

Article 16 is intended to recognize as unethical two basic types of solicitations:

First, telephone or personal solicitations of property owners who have been identified by a real estate sign, multiple listing compilation, or other information service as having exclusively listed their property with another REALTOR®, and

Second, mail or other forms of written solicitations of prospects whose properties are exclusively listed with another REALTOR® when such solicitations are not part of a general mailing but are directed specifically to property owners identified through compilations of current listings, "for sale" or "for rent" signs, or other sources of information required by Article 3 and Multiple Listing Service rules to be made available to other REALTORS® under offers of subagency or cooperation. *(Amended 1/04)*

- Standard of Practice 16-3

    Article 16 does not preclude REALTORS® from contacting the client of another broker for the purpose of offering to provide, or entering into a contract to provide, a different type of real estate service unrelated to the type of service currently being provided (e.g., property management as opposed to brokerage) or from offering the same type of service for property not subject to other brokers' exclusive agreements.

However, information received through a Multiple Listing Service or any other offer of cooperation may not be used to target clients of other REALTORS® to whom such offers to provide services may be made. *(Amended 1/04)*

- Standard of Practice 16-4

REALTORS® shall not solicit a listing which is currently listed exclusively with another broker. However, if the listing broker, when asked by the REALTOR®, refuses to disclose the expiration date and nature of such listing; i.e., an exclusive right to sell, an exclusive agency, open listing, or other form of contractual agreement between the listing broker and the client, the REALTOR® may contact the owner to secure such information and may discuss the terms upon which the REALTOR® might take a future listing or, alternatively, may take a listing to become effective upon expiration of any existing exclusive listing. *(Amended 1/94)*

- Standard of Practice 16-5

REALTORS® shall not solicit buyer/tenant agreements from buyers/ tenants who are subject to exclusive buyer/tenant agreements. However, if asked by a REALTOR®, the broker refuses to disclose the expiration date of the exclusive buyer/tenant agreement, the REALTOR® may contact the buyer/tenant to secure such information and may discuss the terms upon which the REALTOR® might enter into a future buyer/tenant agreement or, alternatively, may enter into a buyer/tenant agreement to become effective upon the expiration of any existing exclusive buyer/tenant agreement. *(Adopted 1/94, Amended 1/98)*

- Standard of Practice 16-6

When REALTORS® are contacted by the client of another REALTOR® regarding the creation of an exclusive relationship to provide the same type of service, and REALTORS® have not directly or indirectly initiated such discussions, they may discuss the terms upon which they might enter into a future agreement or, alternatively, may enter into an agreement which becomes effective upon expiration of any existing exclusive agreement. *(Amended 1/98)*

- Standard of Practice 16-7

The fact that a prospect has retained a REALTOR® as an exclusive representative or exclusive broker in one or more past transactions does not preclude other REALTORS® from seeking such prospect's future business. *(Amended 1/04)*

- Standard of Practice 16-8

The fact that an exclusive agreement has been entered into with a REALTOR® shall not preclude or inhibit any other REALTOR® from entering into a similar agreement after the expiration of the prior agreement. *(Amended 1/98)*

- Standard of Practice 16-9

REALTORS®, prior to entering into a representation agreement, have an affirmative obligation to make reasonable efforts to determine whether the prospect is subject to a current, valid exclusive agreement to provide the same type of real estate service. *(Amended 1/04)*

- Standard of Practice 16-10

REALTORS®, acting as buyer or tenant representatives or brokers, shall disclose that relationship to the seller/landlord's representative or broker at first contact and shall provide written confirmation of that disclosure to the seller/landlord's representative or broker not later than execution of a purchase agreement or lease. *(Amended 1/04)*

- Standard of Practice 16-11

    On unlisted property, REALTORS® acting as buyer/tenant representatives or brokers shall disclose that relationship to the seller/landlord at first contact for that buyer/tenant and shall provide written confirmation of such disclosure to the seller/landlord not later than execution of any purchase or lease agreement. *(Amended 1/04)*

    REALTORS® shall make any request for anticipated compensation from the seller/ landlord at first contact. *(Amended 1/98)*

- Standard of Practice 16-12

    REALTORS®, acting as representatives or brokers of sellers/landlords or as subagents of listing brokers, shall disclose that relationship to buyers/tenants as soon as practicable and shall provide written confirmation of such disclosure to buyers/tenants not later than execution of any purchase or lease agreement. *(Amended 1/04)*

- Standard of Practice 16-13

    All dealings concerning property exclusively listed, or with buyer/tenants who are subject to an exclusive agreement shall be carried on with the client's representative or broker, and not with the client, except with the consent of the client's representative or broker or except where such dealings are initiated by the client.

Before providing substantive services (such as writing a purchase offer or presenting a CMA) to prospects, REALTORS® shall ask prospects whether they are a party to any exclusive representation agreement. REALTORS® shall not knowingly provide substantive services concerning a prospective transaction to prospects who are parties to exclusive representation agreements, except with the consent of the prospects' exclusive representatives or at the direction of prospects. *(Adopted 1/93, Amended 1/04)*

- Standard of Practice 16-14

    REALTORS® are free to enter into contractual relationships or to negotiate with sellers/ landlords, buyers/tenants or others who are not subject to an exclusive agreement but shall not knowingly obligate them to pay more than one commission except with their informed consent. *(Amended 1/98)*

- Standard of Practice 16-15

    In cooperative transactions REALTORS® shall compensate cooperating REALTORS® (principal brokers) and shall not compensate nor offer to compensate, directly or indirectly, any of the sales licensees employed by or affiliated with other REALTORS® without the prior express knowledge and consent of the cooperating broker.

- Standard of Practice 16-16

    REALTORS®, acting as subagents or buyer/tenant representatives or brokers, shall not use the terms of an offer to purchase/lease to attempt to modify the listing broker's offer of compensation to subagents or buyer/tenant representatives or brokers nor make the submission of an executed offer to purchase/lease contingent on the listing broker's agreement to modify the offer of compensation. *(Amended 1/04)*

- Standard of Practice 16-17

  REALTORS®, acting as subagents or as buyer/tenant representatives or brokers, shall not attempt to extend a listing broker's offer of cooperation and/or compensation to other brokers without the consent of the listing broker. *(Amended 1/04)*

- Standard of Practice 16-18

  REALTORS® shall not use information obtained from listing brokers through offers to cooperate made through multiple listing services or through other offers of cooperation to refer listing brokers' clients to other brokers or to create buyer/tenant relationships with listing brokers' clients, unless such use is authorized by listing brokers. *(Amended 1/02)*

- Standard of Practice 16-19

  Signs giving notice of property for sale, rent, lease, or exchange shall not be placed on property without consent of the seller/landlord. *(Amended 1/93)*

- Standard of Practice 16-20

  REALTORS®, prior to or after their relationship with their current firm is terminated, shall not induce clients of their current firm to cancel exclusive contractual agreements between the client and that firm. This does not preclude REALTORS® (principals) from establishing agreements with their associated licensees governing assignability of exclusive agreements. *(Adopted 1/98, Amended 1/10)*

Article 17 (Case Interpretations for Article 17)

In the event of contractual disputes or specific non-contractual disputes as defined in Standard of Practice 17-4 between REALTORS® (principals) associated with different firms, arising out of their relationship as REALTORS®, the REALTORS® shall mediate the dispute if the Board requires its members to mediate. If the dispute is not resolved through mediation, or if mediation is not required, REALTORS® shall submit the dispute to arbitration in accordance with the policies of their Board rather than litigate the matter.

In the event clients of REALTORS® wish to mediate or arbitrate contractual disputes arising out of real estate transactions, REALTORS® shall mediate or arbitrate those disputes in accordance with the policies of the Board, provided the clients agree to be bound by any resulting agreement or award.

The obligation to participate in mediation or arbitration contemplated by this Article includes the obligation of REALTORS® (principals) to cause their firms to mediate or arbitrate and be bound by any resulting agreement or award. *(Amended 1/12)* [listen]

- Standard of Practice 17-1

  The filing of litigation and refusal to withdraw from it by REALTORS® in an arbitrable matter constitutes a refusal to arbitrate. *(Adopted 2/86)*

- Standard of Practice 17-2

  Article 17 does not require REALTORS® to mediate in those circumstances when all parties to the dispute advise the Board in writing that they choose not to mediate through the Board's facilities. The fact that all parties decline to participate in mediation does not relieve REALTORS® of the duty to arbitrate.

Article 17 does not require REALTORS® to arbitrate in those circumstances when all parties to the dispute advise the Board in writing that they choose not to arbitrate before the Board. *(Amended 1/12)*

- Standard of Practice 17-3

    REALTORS®, when acting solely as principals in a real estate transaction, are not obligated to arbitrate disputes with other REALTORS® absent a specific written agreement to the contrary. *(Adopted 1/96)*

- Standard of Practice 17-4

    Specific non-contractual disputes that are subject to arbitration pursuant to Article 17 are:

    1. Where a listing broker has compensated a cooperating broker and another cooperating broker subsequently claims to be the procuring cause of the sale or lease. In such cases the complainant may name the first cooperating broker as respondent and arbitration may proceed without the listing broker being named as a respondent. When arbitration occurs between two (or more) cooperating brokers and where the listing broker is not a party, the amount in dispute and the amount of any potential resulting award is limited to the amount paid to the respondent by the listing broker and any amount credited or paid to a party to the transaction at the direction of the respondent. Alternatively, if the complaint is brought against the listing broker, the listing broker may name the first cooperating broker as a third-party respondent. In either instance the decision of the hearing panel as to

procuring cause shall be conclusive with respect to all current or subsequent claims of the parties for compensation arising out of the underlying cooperative transaction. *(Adopted 1/97, Amended   1/07)*

2. Where a buyer or tenant representative is compensated by the seller or landlord, and not by the listing broker, and the listing broker, as a result, reduces the commission owed by the seller or landlord and, subsequent to such actions, another cooperating broker claims to be the procuring cause of sale or lease. In such cases the complainant may name the first cooperating broker as respondent and arbitration may proceed without the listing broker being named as a respondent. When arbitration occurs between two (or more) cooperating brokers and where the listing broker is not a party, the amount in dispute and the amount of any potential resulting award is limited to the amount paid to the respondent by the seller or landlord and any amount credited or paid to a party to the transaction at the direction of the respondent. Alternatively, if the complaint is brought against the listing broker, the listing broker may name the first cooperating broker as a third-party respondent. In either instance the decision of the hearing panel as to procuring cause shall be conclusive with respect to all current or subsequent claims of the parties for compensation arising out of the underlying cooperative transaction. *(Adopted 1/97, Amended 1/07)*

3. Where a buyer or tenant representative is compensated by the buyer or tenant and, as a result, the listing broker reduces the commission owed by the seller or landlord and, subsequent to such actions, another cooperating broker claims to be the procuring cause of sale or lease. In such cases the complainant may name the first cooperating broker as respondent and arbitration may proceed without the listing broker being named as a respondent. Alternatively, if the complaint is brought against the listing broker, the listing broker may name

the first cooperating broker as a third-party respondent. In either instance the decision of the hearing panel as to procuring cause shall be conclusive with respect to all current or subsequent claims of the parties for compensation arising out of the underlying cooperative transaction. *(Adopted 1/97)*

4. Where two or more listing brokers claim entitlement to compensation pursuant to open listings with a seller or landlord who agrees to participate in arbitration (or who requests arbitration) and who agrees to be bound by the decision. In cases where one of the listing brokers has been compensated by the seller or landlord, the other listing broker, as complainant, may name the first listing broker as respondent and arbitration may proceed between the brokers. *(Adopted   1/97)*

5. Where a buyer or tenant representative is compensated by the seller or landlord, and not by the listing broker, and the listing broker, as a result, reduces the commission owed by the seller or landlord and, subsequent to such actions, claims to be the procuring cause of sale or lease. In such cases arbitration shall be between the listing broker and the buyer or tenant representative and the amount in dispute is limited to the amount of the reduction of commission to which the listing broker agreed. *(Adopted 1/05)*

• Standard of Practice 17-5

The obligation to arbitrate established in Article 17 includes disputes between REALTORS® (principals) in different states in instances where, absent an established inter–association arbitration agreement, the REALTOR® (principal) requesting arbitration agrees to submit to the jurisdiction of, travel to, participate in, and be bound by any resulting award rendered in arbitration conducted by the respondent(s) REALTOR®'s association, in instances where the respondent(s)

REALTOR®'s association determines that an arbitrable issue exists. *(Adopted 1/07)*

Explanatory Notes

The reader should be aware of the following policies which have been approved by the Board of Directors of the National Association:

In filing a charge of an alleged violation of the Code of Ethics by a REALTOR®, the charge must read as an alleged violation of one or more Articles of the Code. Standards of Practice may be cited in support of the charge.

The Standards of Practice serve to clarify the ethical obligations imposed by the various Articles and supplement, and do not substitute for, the Case Interpretations in Interpretations of the Code of Ethics.

Modifications to existing Standards of Practice and additional new Standards of Practice are approved from time to time. Readers are cautioned to ensure that the most recent publications are utilized.

Morning Routine

Your *Morning Routine* is how you prepare yourself to do your best each day. List everything you need to do in the morning to put yourself in a winning mindset. Practice daily and be consistent.

Notes

Notes

Notes

Notes

Notes

Notes

Notes

Notes

Notes

Notes

Notes

Notes

Notes

Notes

Notes

Notes

Notes

Notes

Notes

Notes

Notes

Notes

Notes

Notes

Notes

Notes

Notes

Notes

More about Author

Deborah Ann Spence is an award-winning real estate agent in the state of Pennsylvania, serving clients in Philadelphia and the surrounding suburbs. Born and raised in the Bronx, New York, Spence attended Hofstra University on a full scholarship for inner-city students, called the (NOAH) Program. She graduated in 1994, earning a degree in Business Administration with a major in Accounting and minor in English.

The mother of 2 boys, Spence dealt with a series of medical issues that had her in-and-out of hospitals for nearly a decade before relocating to start over. *The City of Brotherly Love* is where she finally settled and found the opportunity to enter the Real Estate industry.

In an amazing rookie year as an agent, Spence listed 65 homes and sold 31. Proving it was no fluke, she sold nearly 50 more homes in her 2nd year and became a go-to real estate agent (and then, she treated herself to a Mercedes). After reading her success story, you will understand why she says, "If I can do this, so can you."

Spence realizes the key to success is being passionate about learning and having a burning desire to succeed. In this, her 1st book, she offers practical advice, designed to help motivate new real estate agents as they launch, grow their careers, and enjoy the fruits of their hard work.

Made in the USA
Coppell, TX
24 March 2020